Society at a Glance: Asia/Pacific 2019

This work is published on the responsibility of the Secretary-General of the OECD. The opinions expressed and arguments employed herein do not necessarily reflect the official views of the OECD member countries, or those of the World Health Organization.

This document, as well as any data and any map included herein, are without prejudice to the status of or sovereignty over any territory, to the delimitation of international frontiers and boundaries and to the name of any territory, city or area.

Please cite this publication as:
OECD (2019), *Society at a Glance: Asia/Pacific 2019*, OECD Publishing, Paris.
https://doi.org/10.1787/soc_aag-2019-en

ISBN 978-92-64-31087-2 (print)
ISBN 978-92-64-31088-9 (pdf)

Society at a Glance: Asia/Pacific
ISSN 2408-915X (print)
ISSN 2408-9168 (online)

The statistical data for Israel are supplied by and under the responsibility of the relevant Israeli authorities. The use of such data by the OECD is without prejudice to the status of the Golan Heights, East Jerusalem and Israeli settlements in the West Bank under the terms of international law.

Photo credits: © Monkey Business - Fotolia.com; © TheFinalMiracle - Fotolia.com; © Galyna Andrushko - Fotolia.com; © Wolszczak - Fotolia.com; © iStockphoto.com/Eternia; © iStockphoto.com/thinqkreations.

Corrigenda to OECD publications may be found on line at: *www.oecd.org/about/publishing/corrigenda.htm*.

© OECD 2019

You can copy, download or print OECD content for your own use, and you can include excerpts from OECD publications, databases and multimedia products in your own documents, presentations, blogs, websites and teaching materials, provided that suitable acknowledgment of the source and copyright owner is given. All requests for public or commercial use and translation rights should be submitted to *rights@oecd.org*. Requests for permission to photocopy portions of this material for public or commercial use shall be addressed directly to the Copyright Clearance Center (CCC) at *info@copyright.com* or the Centre français d'exploitation du droit de copie (CFC) at *contact@cfcopies.com*.

Foreword

Society at a Glance: Asia/Pacific, *the OECD's overview of social indicators for the region, addresses the growing demand for quantitative evidence on social well-being and its trends across countries in Asia and the Pacific.*

Chapter 1 introduces this volume and provides readers with a guide to help them interpret OECD social indicators. Chapter 2 focuses on issues around extending coverage and the future of social protection in Asia and the Pacific. Many workers in Asia and the Pacific currently have jobs that do not entitle them to social and health support. Digitalization and changes in the nature of work may lead to further job-loss, but also increase economic labour market and economic inequalities between high and low-skilled workers; workers with and without access to social benefits. These rising inequalities will further challenge social policy development in its quest to get support to those who need it most. The chapter includes some country programme examples to illustrate possible policy responses. Chapter 3 to 7 each present 5 indicators on general context, self-sufficiency, equity, health and social cohesion.

A previous draft of this report was discussed at the annual meeting of social policy experts organised by the OECD/Korea policy centre in Seoul on 18- and 19 October 2018. The draft benefitted from comments by the different experts including: Ashish Kumar Aggarwal (India); Shaikh Shamsuddin Ahmed (Bangladesh); Florence Bonnet (ILO); Enkhtsetseg Byambaa (Mongolia); Sri Wening Handayani (ADB); Jai-Joon Hur (Korea); Dohyung Kim (Korea); Norma Binti Mansor (Malaysia); Hina Shaikh (Pakistan); Junko Takezawa (Japan); Turro Wongkaren (Indosnesia); and, Suk-myung Yun (Korea).

This report was prepared by Willem Adema, Pauline Fron, and Eunkyung Shin. Peter Whiteford (Australia National University) prepared parts of Chapter 2, while the contribution of data on informality by Florence Bonnet (ILO) and Social Expenditure by Sri Wening Handayani (ADB) is gratefully acknowledged. Maxime Ladaique (Fertility) and Philippe Herve (International Migration) contributed to Chapter 3; Andrew Reilly provided data on pensions for Chapter 5, while Luca Lorenzoni and Frédéric Daniel provided data and comments on Chapter 7. We are grateful for comments on previous drafts by Daniel Alonso Soto, Mark Pearson, Monika Queisser, Stefano Scarpetta, Stefan Thewissen, and the many other colleagues who provided assistance including Liv Gudmundson, Lucy Hulett, Anna Irvin Sigal and Fatima Perez.

The on-line version of this publication, including all figures and data, can be accessed via http://oe.cd/sag-asia.

Table of contents

Follow OECD Publications on:

http://twitter.com/OECD_Pubs

http://www.facebook.com/OECDPublications

http://www.linkedin.com/groups/OECD-Publications-4645871

http://www.youtube.com/oecdilibrary

http://www.oecd.org/oecddirect/

This book has... *StatLinks*
A service that delivers Excel® files from the printed page!

Look for the *StatLinks* at the bottom of the tables or graphs in this book. To download the matching Excel® spreadsheet, just type the link into your Internet browser, starting with the *http://dx.doi.org* prefix, or click on the link from the e-book edition.

Acronyms and conventional signs

Asia/Pacific countries and economies ISO codes

Armenia	ARM
Azerbaijan	AZE
Bangladesh	BGD
Bhutan	BTN
Brunei Darussalam	BRN
Cambodia	KHM
China	CHN
Fiji	FJI
Hong Kong, China	HKG
India	IND
Indonesia	IDN
Kazakhstan	KAZ
Korea Democratic People's Republic (hereafter Korea DPR)	PRK
Kyrgyz Republic	KGZ
Lao People's Democratic Republic (hereafter Lao PDR)	LAO
Macau, China	MAC
Malaysia	MYS
Maldives	MDV
Mongolia	MNG
Myanmar	NMR
Nepal	NPL
Pakistan	PAK
Papua New Guinea	PNG
Philippines	PHL
Samoa	WSM
Singapore	SGP
Sri Lanka	LKA
Tajikistan	TJK
Thailand	THA
Timor-Leste	TLS
Tonga	TON
Viet Nam	VNM

OECD Asia/Pacific countries ISO Codes

Australia	AUS
Japan	JPN
Korea	KOR
New Zealand	NZL

Asia/Pacific refers to all countries for which data are shown, including OECD members Australia, Japan, Korea and New Zealand when relevant.

Conventional signs

.. or n.a: Not available.

(↘) in the legend relates to the variable for which countries are ranked from left to right in decreasing order.

(↗) in the legend relates to the variable for which countries are ranked from left to right in increasing order.

Society at a Glance
Asia/Pacific 2019
© OECD 2019

Executive summary

Society at a Glance Asia/Pacific 2019 presents 25 key indicators on general socio-economic context, self-sufficiency, equity, health and social cohesion for 36 countries and territories in Asia and the Pacific. The report also includes a chapter focusing on the issues associated to the extension of coverage and the future of social protection in the region.

Economic growth has been substantial across Asia and the Pacific in recent years, but it has not always been inclusive

Over the 2013-2017 period, countries in the region grew at 4.4% on average in real terms. For comparison, this is twice as high as the OECD average. Substantial economic growth across Asia and the Pacific over the past 10 years has contributed to a decline in absolute poverty as the share of people with incomes below USD 1.9 per day has almost halved to 6.0%. Nevertheless, income inequality remains high, – the Gini coefficient on income inequality is around 0.36 on average in Asia and Pacific countries as compared with 0.32 in the OECD area.

Public social expenditure and tax revenue remain low in Asia and the Pacific

Social protection systems are underdeveloped in most countries of the region. Public social expenditure across Asia and the Pacific was just 7% of GDP in 2015, compared with 21% of GDP on average in the OECD countries. Furthermore, the redistributive power of social spending is limited as most of it concerns payments to (former) workers with a formal employment contract – a group that is relatively well-off compared to those in the informal sector. The differences in social spending levels between the Asia/Pacific region and the OECD are mirrored in different tax revenues: In Australia, Japan, Korea and New Zealand the tax-to-GDP ratio ranged from 26 to 33%, while in Indonesia, Kazakhstan, Malaysia, Papua New Guinea, the Philippines, Singapore and Thailand they were between 12 and 18% in 2016.

Informal employment is widespread across most of Asia and the Pacific

The share of informal employment varies across countries, but almost 70% of workers in the Asia/Pacific region are in informal employment, often self-employed without employees (own-account workers) and/or contributory family workers (especially in low-income countries), often working long hours for little money and in jobs that are not covered by social protection and health insurance. Youths (age 15-24) and elderly workers (over age 65) are most likely to be in informal employment. Only 30% of those with tertiary education work informally. Across Asia and the Pacific, the informal economy absorbs a large share of low-skilled workers, partly explaining its low overall level of productivity.

Digitalisation and changes in the nature of work and labour markets can further challenge social protection development

The already considerable challenge of extending social protection coverage to informal workers is exacerbated by changes in the nature of work and labour markets. In some economies in developing Asia, about half of the jobs could be affected by automation: some may disappear altogether while many others will be transformed. Many of the low-productivity jobs in Asia and the Pacific are technically "automatable" but automation may not be economically attractive given relatively low wages and high costs of investment in ICT. However, as automation will increase the demand for higher skills there is a real possibility of further labour market polarisation and increased economic inequality in the future. The response to this challenge is to increase investment in education and training in order to develop the appropriate skills for jobs complementing the new technology.

Technological advancements can also help administration of benefits and their delivery

The digital transformation also provides new opportunities for the extension of social protection as they can help overcome some of the administrative barriers to the receipt of benefit, payment of taxes and social security contributions. Advances in technology have at least the potential to contribute to a reduction in informality and the improvement of benefit delivery. This is important for the countries in Asia such as Bangladesh, China, India, Indonesia and Pakistan with very large populations as well as countries in the Pacific with very small populations, as in both cases natural environments pose challenges to the development, implementation and administration of social programmes.

Population ageing is another social policy challenge affecting many countries in the region

Population ageing is an another important policy challenge, particularly in North East Asia, where rapid increases in life expectancy and even more rapid declines in fertility have resulted in the fastest rates of population ageing in history. At the same time, traditional family ties are weakening, leaving gaps in social protection that need to be addressed quickly. A further factor is that rapid income and wage growth can lead to wide gaps emerging between the retired and those working in the newer and more prosperous economy.

Scaling up social investment and increasing tax revenue is needed to effectively combat poverty

Countries in Asia and Pacific should do more to protect poor families from poverty. This includes scaling up investment in social protection systems, better targeting of supports, and where possible linking these with existing education, health and employment policies. Countries could build on the existing social protection infrastructure, but given the low level of spending and taxation overall, widening the tax base and greater progressivity in taxation and financing of social insurance schemes would help to make national tax/benefit systems more effective in combating poverty.

OECD/Korea Policy Centre

The Joint OECD/Korea Policy Centre (*www.oecdkorea.org*) is an international co-operation organisation established by a Memorandum of Understanding between the OECD and the Government of the Republic of Korea. The Centre – officially opened in 2008 – results from the integration of 4 pre-existing OECD/Korea Centres, one of which was the Regional Centre on Health and Social Policy (RCHSP), established in 2005.

The major functions of the Centre are to research international standards and policies on international taxation, competition, public governance, and social and health policy sectors in OECD member economies and to disseminate research outcomes to public officials and experts in the region. In the area of health and social policy, the Centre promotes policy dialogue and information sharing between OECD economies and non-OECD Asian/Pacific countries.

There are four main areas of work: social protection statistics (jointly with the International Labour Organisation and the Asian Development Bank); the Family Database for the Asia/Pacific region; health expenditure and financing statistics, quality of care indicators and policies to improve affordability of medicines (jointly with the World Health Organisation) and on pension policies (jointly with the World Bank). In pursuit of this vision, the Centre hosts various kinds of educational programme, international meetings, seminars, and workshops in each sector and provides policy forums presented by experts at home and abroad.

Society at a Glance
Asia/Pacific 2019
© OECD 2019

Chapter 1

Introduction to Society at a Glance Asia/Pacific

The *Society at a Glance Asia/Pacific* series provides an example of how OECD frameworks may be used to highlight and illustrate societal progress and social policy issues in the Asia/Pacific region (OECD, 2014[1]). The purpose of *Society at a Glance Asia/Pacific* and *Society at Glance* series more generally[1] is to provide information on two questions:

- Compared with their own past and with other countries, what progress have countries made in their social development?
- How effective have been societies' efforts to further their own development?

Addressing the first question about societal progress requires indicators that cover a broad range of social outcomes across countries and over time. As social development requires improvements in health, education and economic resources, as well as a stable basis for social interactions, indicators have to be found for all these dimensions.

The second question about societal effectiveness is even more challenging to answer. Societies try to influence social outcomes, often through government policy. Whether policies are effective in achieving their aims is a critical issue. Indicators help to make that assessment. A first step is to compare the resources intended to change outcomes across countries and contrast those resources with social outcomes. While this comparison is far from being a comprehensive evaluation of policy effectiveness, indicators can contribute to highlighting areas where more evaluative work may be needed.

Building on the OECD report *A Decade of Social Protection Development in Selected Asian Countries* (OECD, 2017[2]), this issue special's chapter discusses issues around extending coverage and the future of social protection in Asia and the Pacific. The important challenge of extending social protection coverage to informal workers is exacerbated by changes in the nature of work due to automation, and apart from the risks of job-loss, there are growing concerns about increasing labour market polarisation and economic inequality. However, technological advancements can also help overcome some of the barriers to the receipt of benefit and payment of taxes and social security contributions. These opportunities need to be explored to as scaling up social investment and increasing tax revenue is needed to effectively combat poverty.

The framework of OECD social indicators

The structure applied here is not a full-scale framework of social indicators. But it is more than a simple list of indicators. This framework has been informed by experiences in other parts of the OECD on policy and outcome assessment in a variety of fields. It draws, in particular, on the OECD experience with environmental indicators. The indicators are based on a variant of the "Pressure-State-Response" (PSR) framework that has also been used in other policy areas (United Nations, 1996[3]). In this framework human activities exert ***pressures*** on the environment, which affect the ***state*** of natural resources and environmental conditions, and which prompt a ***societal response*** to these changes through various policies. The PSR framework highlights these sequential links, which in turn helps decision-makers and the public to interconnections that are often overlooked.

A similar approach for social indicators is followed in this report. Indicators are grouped along two dimensions their nature and the policy fields that they cover. The first dimension is broken down into three areas:

- ***Social context*** refers to variables that, while not usually direct policy targets, are crucial for understanding the social policy context. For example, the proportion of elderly people in the total population is not a policy target. However, it is relevant information about the social landscape in which, for example, health, taxation or pension policy responses are made. Unlike other indicators, trends in social context indicators cannot be unambiguously interpreted as "good" or "bad".
- ***Social status*** indicators describe the social outcomes that policies try to influence. These indicators describe the general conditions of the population. Ideally, the indicators chosen are ones that can be easily and unambiguously interpreted – all countries would rather have low poverty rates than high ones, for example.
- ***Societal response*** indicators provide information about what society is doing to affect social status indicators. Societal responses include indicators of government policy settings. Additionally, the activities of non-governmental organisations, families and the broader civil society also involve societal responses. Comparing societal response indicators with social status indicators provides an initial indication of policy effectiveness.

An important limitation of the social context, social status and societal response indicators used here is that these are presented at a national level. For countries with a significant degree of federalism and/or regional variation, Australia, China or India such indicators may not be reflective of the different regions within the federation, which may have different contexts, outcomes and social responses. This limitation should be borne in mind in considering the indicators presented below.

In addition, the framework used in *Society at a Glance Asia/Pacific* groups "social status" and "social response" indicators according to the broad policy fields that they cover:

1. ***Self-sufficiency*** is an underlying objective of social policy. Self-sufficiency is promoted by ensuring people's active social and economic participation, and their autonomy in activities of daily life.
2. ***Equity*** is another longstanding objective of social policy. Equitable outcomes are measured mainly in terms of access by people and families to resources.
3. ***Health*** status is a fundamental objective of health care systems, but improving health status also requires a wider focus on its social determinants, making health a central objective of social policy.
4. ***Social cohesion*** is often identified as an over-arching objective of countries' social policies. While little agreement exists on what it means, a range of symptoms are informative about a lack of social cohesion. Social cohesion is more positively evident in the extent to which people participate in their communities.

The selection and description of indicators

Asia/Pacific countries differ substantially in the ways that they collect and publish social indicators. In selecting indicators for this report, the following questions were considered.

- What is the minimum degree of indicator comparability across countries? This report strives to present the best comparative information for each of the areas covered.

However, the indicators presented are not confined to those for which there is "absolute" comparability. Readers are, however, alerted as to the nature of the data used and the limits to comparability.

- What is the minimum number of countries for which the data must be available? This report generally includes only indicators that are available for a majority of countries.
- What decompositions should be used at a country level? Social indicators can often be disaggregated at a national level into outcomes by social sub-categories, as for example people's age. Pragmatism prevails: the decompositions presented here vary according to the indicator considered. Individual indicators can be relevant for multiple areas of social policy. That is to say, they could plausibly be included under more than one category. For example, the ability to undertake activities of daily living without assistance is potentially an indicator of social cohesion, self-sufficiency and health. Indicators are presented here under the category for which they are considered to be most relevant.

General social context indicators

When comparing social status and societal response indicators, it is easy to suggest that one country is doing badly relative to others, or that another is spending a lot of money in a particular area compared with others. It is important to put such statements into a broader context. For example, national income levels vary across OECD countries. If there is any link between income and health, richer countries may have better health conditions than poor ones, irrespectively of societal responses. If the demand for health care services increases with income (as appears to be the case), rich countries may spend more on health care (as a percentage of national income) than poorer countries. These observations do not mean that the indicators of health status and health spending are misleading. They do mean, however, that the general context behind the data should be borne in mind when considering policy implications.

General social context indicators, including fertility, marriage and divorce, migration and the old age support ratio, provide the general background for the other indicators in this report. GDP per capita is a social outcome in its own right, giving an indication of the average material well-being of that society.

Table 1.1. **List of general context indicators**

GDP per capita
Fertility
Marriage and divorce
International migration
Old-age support ratio

Self-sufficiency indicators

For many people, paid active labour force participation and employment provide income, identity and social interactions. Hence promoting higher labour force participation and paid employment is a priority for most countries. A better education enables longer term self-sufficiency now and in the future, including in paid employment. Early childhood education provides a foundation for future learning, as well as freeing up mothers to choose to work. Educational attainment and students performance provides information on human capital accumulation. Education spending provides information on the primary social response made by governments to help ensure self-sufficiency. The reader should keep that these self-sufficiency indicators are also related to equity indicators, such as employment, pensions and social spending.

Table 1.2. **List of self-sufficiency indicators**

Social status	Societal responses
Labour force participation	Education spending
Employment	
Early childhood education and care	
Educational attainment and student performance	

Equity

Equity has many dimensions. It concerns the ability to access social services and economic opportunities, as well as equity in outcomes. Opinions vary widely as to what exactly entails a fair or a just distribution of opportunities. Additionally, as it is hard to obtain information on all dimensions of equity, the social status equity indicators are focussed on inequality in financial resources.

Table 1.3. **List of equity indicators**

Social status	Societal responses
Poverty	Public social expenditure
Income inequality	Solidarity
	Pensions: coverage and replacement rates

Poverty is a natural starting point for considering equity at the bottom of society. Absolute measures of poverty are used here, since many of the region's countries are very poor. In addition to an absolute poverty measure, an indicator of relative inequality across the distribution is also considered. Pension coverage and the old-age replacement rate are important indicators of the extent to which society treats its older people in an equitable fashion. Many Asia/Pacific countries have social protection systems that redistribute resources and insure people against various contingencies. These interventions are summarised by public social spending, while the solidarity indicator reflects on the extent to which people make donations and/or participate in voluntary work.

Health

The links between social and health conditions are strong. Indeed, educational gains, accompanied by public health measures, better access to health care and continuing progress in medical technology, have contributed to significant improvements in health status, as measured by life expectancy. To a significant extent, improvements in life expectancy reflect lower infant mortality. As it is essential for economic development and well-being to access sufficient, safe, nutritious food and balanced diet, child malnutrition is a salient indicator to predict a country's economic and social development potential.

Health expenditure is a general and key part of the policy response of health care systems to concerns about health conditions. The indicator on hospital activities provides information on the number of hospital beds, discharge rates and duration of stays in hospitals. Nevertheless, health problems are frequently rooted in interrelated social conditions – such as unemployment, poverty and inadequate housing – that are beyond the reach of health policies.

Table 1.4. **List of health indicators**

Social status	Societal responses
Life expectancy	Health expenditure
Infant and child mortality	Hospital activities
Child malnutrition	

Social cohesion

Promoting social cohesion is an important social policy goal in many countries. However, because there is no commonly-accepted definition, identifying suitable indicators is particularly difficult. The approach taken here in *Society at a Glance Asia/Pacific* is to assess social cohesion through indicators that describe the extent to which citizens participate in societal life trust their fellow citizens and institutions, and derive satisfaction from their daily activities.

Table 1.5. **List of social cohesion indicators**

Social status	Societal responses
Life satisfaction	
Confidence in institutions	
Trust and safety	
Tolerance	
Voting	

Life satisfaction is strongly associated with confidence in the broader society and its institutions. A general measure of trust in other people and safety may indicate the degree to which economic and social exchange is facilitated, enhancing well-being and facilitating socially productive collective action. The degree of community acceptance of minority groups (migrants, ethnic minorities and gay and lesbian people) is a measurable dimension of social cohesion. Finally, high voter turnout indicates that a country's political system enjoys a high level of participation, increasing its effectiveness and reflecting a broad public consensus about its legitimacy.

What can be found in this publication?

The next chapter discusses issues around extending coverage and the future of social protection in Asia and the Pacific. Chapters 3 to 7 cover each of the five domains of social indicators as discussed above. For each indicator, there is a page of text and a page of figures. Both figures and text are, to a degree, standardised. Both the text and figures address the most recent headline indicator data, with country performances often ranked from best to worst. Changes in the indicator over time and the length of the time-period at hand can be considered when data are available. Having addressed the indicator and changes over time, the text and figures then typically consider an alternative disaggregation of the indicator, or relationships with other social outcomes or policies. For each indicator, a boxed section on "Definition and measurement" provides the definitions of the data used and a discussion of potential measurement issues. Finally, suggestions for further reading can be given.

Note

1. A related OECD publication, *How's life? 2017 – Measuring Well-being* (OECD, 2017[4]), presents the latest evidence from 50 indicators, covering both current well-being outcomes and resources for future well-being, and including changes since 2005. Compared with Society at a Glance, it uses a broader set of outcome measures but excludes indicators of policy responses.

References

OECD (2017), *A Decade of Social Protection Development in Selected Asian Countries*, OECD Publishing, Paris, *http://dx.doi.org/10.1787/9789264272262-en*. [2]

OECD (2017), *How's Life? 2017: Measuring Well-being*, OECD Publishing, Paris, *https://dx.doi.org/10.1787/how_life-2017-en*. [4]

OECD (2014), *Society at a Glance: Asia/Pacific 2014*, OECD Publishing, Paris, *https://dx.doi.org/10.1787/9789264220553-en*. [1]

United Nations (1996), "Glossary of Environment Statistics", *F*, No. 67, Department for Economic and Social Information and Policy Analysis, Studies in Methods, *https://unstats.un.org/unsd/publication/SeriesF/SeriesF_67E.pdf* (accessed on 29 November 2018). [3]

Society at a Glance
Asia/Pacific 2019
© OECD 2019

Chapter 2

Extending coverage and the future of social protection in Asia and the Pacific

Introduction

Economic growth has been substantial over the past decade, and while it has contributed to an overall reduction in absolute poverty, wide income disparities persist in Asia and the Pacific.

At present social protection systems in Asia and the Pacific remain underdeveloped: at 7% of GDP, public social spending in Asia and the Pacific is low. Moreover, most social spending is through social insurance schemes that cover (former) workers with a formal employment contract who generally belong to middle and higher-income groups. The share of informal employment in total employment varies across countries, but almost 70% of workers in the Asia/Pacific region are in informal employment, often the self-employed without employees (own-account workers) and/or contributory family workers, who often work long hours for little money and without or only limited access to social protection.

Changes in automation and the rise of the "platform economy" are widely recognised as posing challenges to labour markets across the OECD as well as Asia and the Pacific. However, developments in technology and automation also provide new opportunities for the extension of social protection as they can help overcome some of the administrative barriers to the receipt of benefit, payment of taxes and social security contributions. Advances in technology have at least the potential to contribute to a reduction in informality and the improvement of benefit delivery.

More should be done to support the poor, which requires scaling up investment in social-support systems and better targeting of supports. This chapter includes a selection of reform efforts across the region to increase coverage social protection. But given the low level of spending and taxation overall, widening the tax base and greater progressivity in taxation and financing of social insurance schemes would be important contributory factors to a greater effectiveness of national policies to combat poverty.

Strong growth, but social expenditure is low in Asia/Pacific

Economies in Asia/Pacific often enjoy steady economic and employment growth

Economies in the Asia/Pacific region continue to grow faster than OECD economies. Over the 2013-2017 period, countries in the region experienced strong economic growth at 4.4% on average in real terms): a growth rate that is twice as high as across the OECD on average (OECD, 2018[1]). Among OECD countries in the region over the same period, growth was most pronounced in New Zealand (3.5%), while Korea (3%) and Australia (2.5%) also performed above the OECD average: at just over 1% per annum over the past five years economic growth in Japan was sluggish (Figure 2.1). By contrast, economic powerhouses such as China (7.1%), India (7.1%) and Indonesia (5.1%) continued to enjoy strong growth trends since 2013. Smaller and often relatively poor economies, such as Bangladesh, Bhutan, Cambodia, Lao PDR, Myanmar, the Philippines, Tajikistan and Viet Nam also experienced annual growth rates of around 6-7% over the 2013-17 period (ADB, 2018[2]).

Figure 2.1. **Strong growth is expected to continue in Asia/Pacific**

Real GDP growth, per cent per year

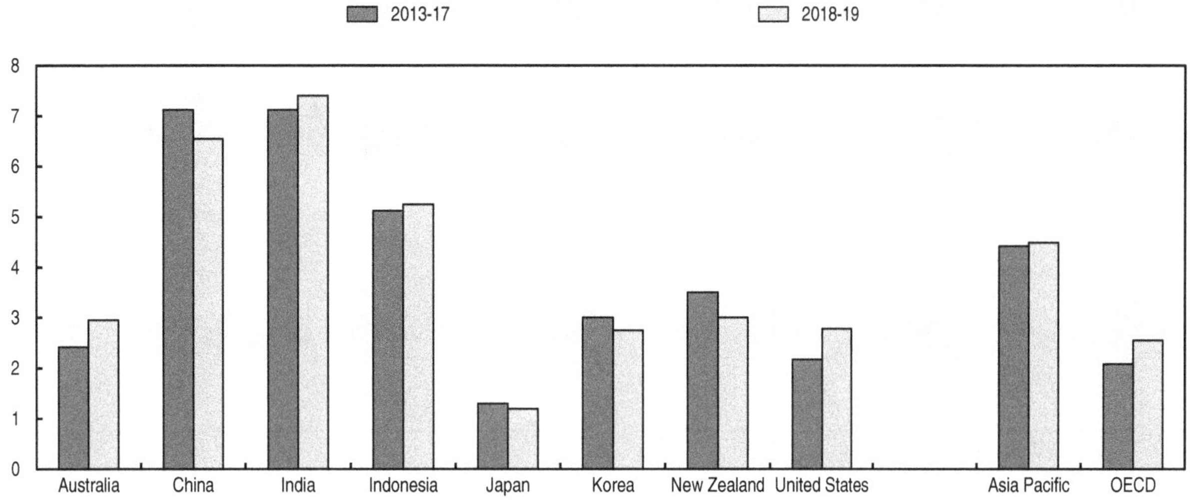

Source: ADB (2018), Asian Development Outlook 2018: How Technology Affects Jobs, *www.adb.org/publications/asian-development-outlook-2018-how-technology-affects-jobs*; OECD (2018), *OECD Economic Outlook*, Volume 2018, Issue 1, *https://dx.doi.org/10.1787/eco_outlook-v2018-1-en*; and, OECD (2018), *OECD Interim Economic Outlook*, September, *www.oecd.org/economy/outlook/economic-outlook/*.

StatLink *http://dx.doi.org/10.1787/888933899584*

The outlook for 2018 and 2019 for many economies in the region is to continue to enjoy steady growth (Figure 2.1). The growth rate in China is anticipated to slow down as it is in Central Asia and the pacific (ADB, 2018[2]) Growth in India is projected to stay strong, and Southeast Asia is projected to maintain its growth momentum, averaging 5.2% per year from 2018 to 2022 (OECD, 2018[3]). However, there are risks, including an escalation of trade tensions which might significantly affect the economic expansion, while persistently high oil-prices will increase inflationary pressures and could aggravate external imbalances in many countries (OECD, 2018[1]). Also, the increase of wage costs over the past decade in China and elsewhere in Asia has eroded the previous benefits of "offshoring", and in some cases have contributed to s shift back of production to the country of origin, as, for example, Philips Electronics that shifted production back from China to the Netherlands in 2012 (World Bank Group, 2018[4]).

Notwithstanding concerns about income inequality and future employment growth, strong past economic growth in the Asia/Pacific region, has contributed to important progress in reducing extreme poverty. Over the past decade: the share of people living in extreme poverty – with incomes below USD 1.9 per day, has almost halved to 6.0% across the Asia/Pacific region, see *Indicator* 5.1. *Poverty* (throughout the chapter there are references to Indicators that are included in Chapters 3, 4, 5, 6 and 7 of this volume). The reduction in extreme poverty over the past 10 years was most pronounced in China, Indonesia, India, Timor-Leste and Viet Nam.

Social expenditure and tax revenue are relatively low

Welfare states in OECD countries have developed over many years. Back in 1960, public social expenditure ranged from 5-10% of GDP in Japan and the United States, and 10-15% of GDP in Australia, France, Sweden, and New Zealand (Figure 2.2). Over the years, public social expenditure (Box 2.1) has ratcheted up with crises in the early 1970s, 1980s, early 1990s and most recently the Great Recession that blew up in 2007/8. In addition to economic crisis

Figure 2.2. **Welfare states in OECD countries took a long time to develop**

Trends in public social protection spending as a percent of GDP, 1960-2018

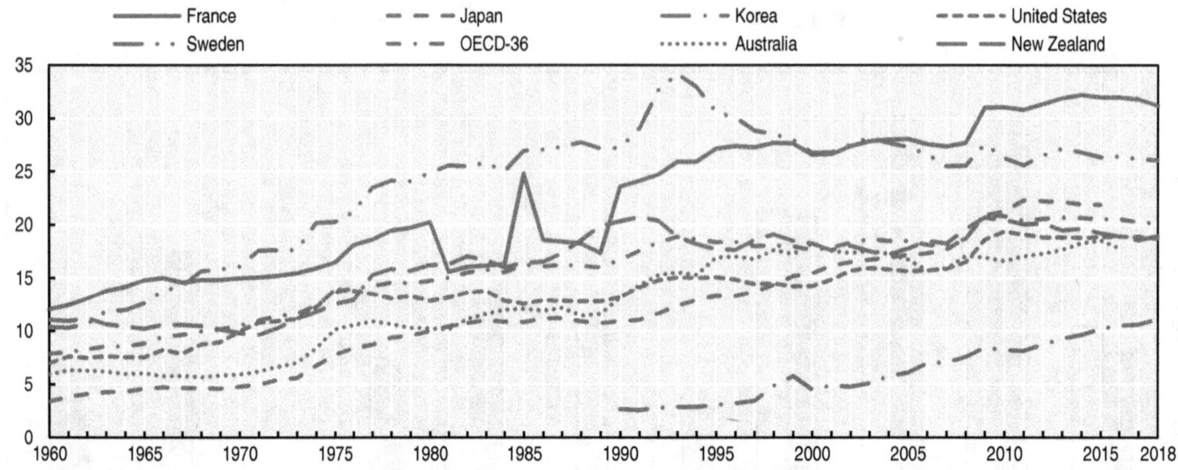

Source: OECD (2019), Social Expenditure Database (SOCX), *www.oecd.org/social/expenditure.htm*.

StatLink http://dx.doi.org/10.1787/888933899603

Box 2.1. **Defining social expenditure**

The OECD defines social expenditures as "the provision by public and private institutions of benefits to, and financial contributions targeted at, households and individuals in order to provide support during circumstances which adversely affect their welfare, provided that the provision of the benefits and financial contributions constitutes neither a direct payment for a particular good or service nor an individual contract or transfer." Transfers between households – albeit of a social nature, are not: this is important as in the Asia/ Pacific region support between family members (often living together) is a central part of the social fabric (Adema, Fron and Ladaique, 2011[5]).

Broadly speaking there are two main criteria that have to be simultaneously satisfied for a programme to be classified as social: the programme has to redistribute resources across people and has to serve a social purpose (OECD, 2019[6]). The inter-personal redistribution of resources is often brought about by compulsory participation or by public financing of social benefits. The extent of redistribution can also be determined by programme characteristics as benefit caps, increased contribution rates for workers with higher earnings, and is most evident when support is provided for free, e.g. free medical aid or the provision of income support under minimum living standard schemes such as in China, Japan or Korea.

There are different categorizations of social support (OECD, 2019[6]; ADB, 2018[2]; Eurostat, 2016[7]; ILO, 2005[8]), but benefits with a social purpose generally include: support for the elderly and pensions for-old-age and/or survivors; incapacity related benefits, including invalidity benefits, benefits accruing from occupational injury and accident legislation, and employee sickness payments; family benefits – child allowances, childcare support, and income support during maternity leave; housing allowances; unemployment benefits and active labour market policies – e.g. training, direct job creation, and start-up incentives; and, health supports as in- and out-patient care, medical goods, and health prevention.

inducing increased spending on unemployment compensation, social assistance and active labour market policies as well as a decline in GDP (the denominator in the spending-to-GDP ratios), population ageing in OECD countries is driving up social spending through increased health and pension expenditures. With population ageing and increased spending on health and pension insurance benefits social spending in Japan has increased to 21.9% of GDP. Population ageing is less pronounced in Australia and New Zealand while income-testing in social protection systems of these countries has limited growth of social spending over the years: in both countries public social spending was just below 20% of GDP in 2017. In Korea, a much younger welfare state, public social spending amounted to just over 10% in 2015, just like in many western-European OECD countries back in the mid-1960s. However, population ageing will unfold much more rapidly in Korea, and Korean policymakers will have less time to put adequate social protection provisions in place than their western-European peers had (*see Indicator 3.5, Old-age support ratio*).

Compared with on average 20% across the OECD in 2016/8, public social expenditure across Asia and the /Pacific is relatively low at 7% of GDP in 2015 (Figure 2.3). Public social spending in Australia, Japan and New Zealand is at least around 20% of GDP, and around 10% in Korea and Mongolia. In Bangladesh, Bhutan, Cambodia, Hong Kong, China, India, Indonesia, Lao PDR, Myanmar, Pakistan, Papua New Guinea and the Philippines, public social spending amounted to less than half the average for the Asia/Pacific region.

Figure 2.3. **Public social spending in Asia/Pacific is about one-third of the OECD average**

Public social expenditure as a percent of GDP, 2017 or most recent year

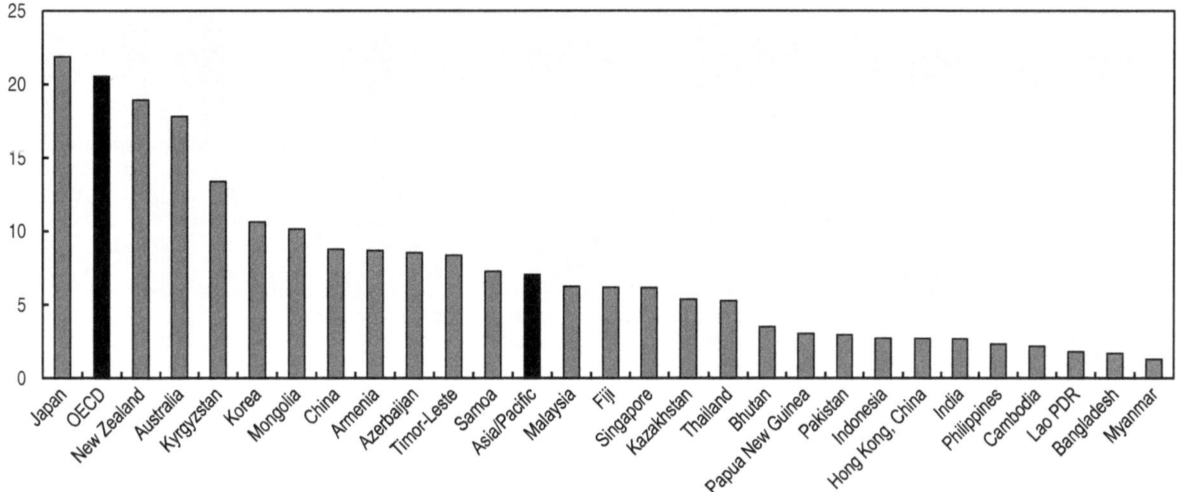

Note: See notes and sources to *Indicator Public Social Expenditure*.

StatLink http://dx.doi.org/10.1787/888933899622

Most Asia/Pacific countries have introduced statutory social expenditure programmes towards employment injuries, disability and support in old-age. However, financial support in the case of sickness, maternity and unemployment sometimes critically depends on employer financing, and about one-third of the countries in the region do not have statutory provisions towards family allowances (ILO, 2017[9]). In practice, however, social protection systems provide limited supports, as coverage is often limited to only a small portion of workers and the (working-age) population (see below). The relatively low level of public social spending implies that a large number of people in many countries are vulnerable to contingencies that adversely affect their welfare such as poverty, illness, disability and unemployment receive little or no support.

The differences in social spending levels between Asian countries and OECD countries are mirrored in differences in tax revenues (Figure 2.4 and (OECD, 2018[10]; OECD, 2018[11]). In 2016, the tax-to-GDP ratio across the OECD on average was 34%, and in many European countries the tax intake was considerably higher: tax-to-GDP ratios were highest in France and Denmark at almost 46% (OECD, 2018[10]). Tax-to-GDP ratios among OECD countries in the Asia/Pacific region remain below the OECD average even though having increased by 3 to 4 percentage points since 2010 in Australia, Japan, Korea and New Zealand (OECD, 2018[11]). Tax-to-GDP ratios in Indonesia, Kazakhstan, Malaysia, Papua New Guinea, the Philippines, Singapore and Thailand are lower still and ranged from 11.6 to 18.1% of GDP in 2016; the recent decline in Kazakhstan was largely due to a fall in oil tax revenue (OECD, 2018[11]).

Figure 2.4. **Tax revenue in Asian countries is well below the OECD average**

Tax revenue to GDP ratios, 2005 and 2016

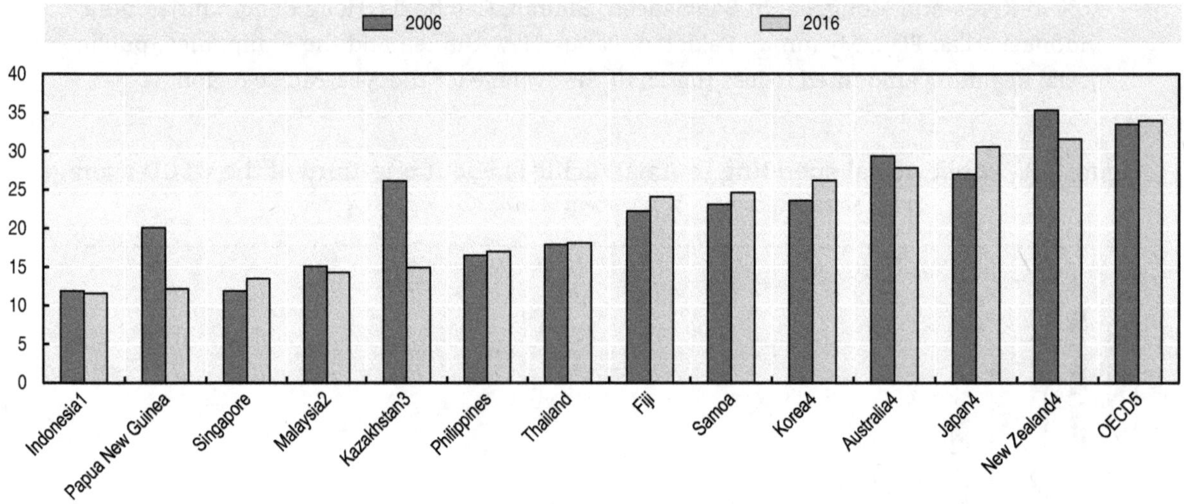

1. Data on social security contributions are not available but they are thought to be negligible as they relate only to the "Asuransi Kesehatan" – a health insurance programme for employees in for-profit state-owned enterprises.
2. Figures do not include tax revenues from local governments (Quit Rent and Assessment tax), which are unavailable.
3. The data are estimated for 2016 (social security contributions).
4. Data for Australia, Japan, Korea, New Zealand and the OECD average are taken from the OECD Revenue Statistics 2018.
5. Represents an unweighted average for the 36 OECD countries in the OECD Revenue Statistics 2018.

Source: OECD (2018), Revenue Statistics 2018, *https://doi.org/10.1787/rev_stats-2018-en* and OECD (2018), Revenue Statistics in Asian and Pacific Economies, *https://dx.doi.org/10.1787/9789264308091-en*.

StatLink *http://dx.doi.org/10.1787/888933899641*

The relatively low tax-to-GDP levels suggest that there is space to increase tax receipt to enhance social expenditure. ADB (2016[12]) suggests that in the majority of Asian countries a basic level of social protection can be provided without introducing high levels of taxation, and that major gaps in social protection can be closed by increased spending worth 2 to 3% of GDP. Re-allocation of resources within national budgets, increasing taxation and improving tax collection can all contribute to creating the necessary budget space for improved social spending. Recent developments in information and communication technology (ICT), both for electronic filing and for payment of taxes, have presented many opportunities for revenue bodies to increase government revenue, improve efficiency, and enhance the quality of services delivered to taxpayers. At the same time, ICT-development has enabled an overall reduction in taxpayer compliance costs and government administration costs, while delivering improved enforcement (OECD, 2017[13]).

Income inequality is high in the Asia/Pacific region compared with the OECD and income disparities seem widest in Malaysia and China (*see Indicator 5.2, Income Inequality*). As both public social spending and tax revenue are relatively low, the overall redistribution of resources though tax/benefit systems in Asia and the Pacific is limited compared to OECD countries (Adema, Fron and Ladaique, 2014$_{[14]}$). Tax bases are small and the nature of tax systems is limited in progressivity.

Moreover, while contributory social insurance programmes account for the bulk of public social spending in many counties in Asia and the Pacific (ADB, forthcoming$_{[15]}$), their coverage, by definition, is limited to formal workers: i.e. those who are comparatively well-off. However, even among formal workers in the Asia/Pacific region, the effectiveness of social insurance can be limited due to the combination of patchy coverage, the lack of unemployment insurance, and/or relatively low payment rates. As a result, the impact of social insurance benefits on the income distribution tends to be regressive whereas such benefits typically have a strong inequality-reducing effect in more advanced economies (Adema, Fron and Ladaique, 2014$_{[14]}$). In all, social protection systems in Asia and the Pacific need to be further developed to effectively combat poverty in the region.

Technological progress will continue to contribute to growth but there are displacement risks for manual and routine jobs

Economic growth has contributed to strong job creation in Asia: ADB (2018$_{[2]}$) asserts that over the past 25 years, the region has created 30 million jobs annually in industry and services. Investment in education, infrastructure, international trade, foreign investment, a favourable business climate and macroeconomic stability have all contributed to the adoption of new technology and the associated job creation. Technological progress has improved productivity in low-productivity sectors (subsistence agriculture), and also contributed to an overall shift away from agriculture to service sectors with higher productivity and pay. Some countries in east Asia, such as Viet Nam or Lao PDR, have managed to upgrade their human capital, expand the manufacturing sector and have young skilled workers apply new technology to upgrade manufacturing production and generate future growth on that basis (World Bank Group, 2018$_{[4]}$).[1]

In other countries future employment growth will have to rely predominantly on service sector development and the wider application of ICT in it. Many Asian economies are well placed as, for example, internet use, a prerequisite for participation in much of the activity in the digital economy, has increased across the region in recent years, and in China, the Philippines, Thailand and Viet Nam about 40 to 50% of the population are regular internet users and this is close to 80% in Malaysia and Singapore (OECD, 2018$_{[3]}$). However, while the manufacturing sector involves a considerable share of low- and medium skilled jobs, service sector employment growth in ICT or finance is likely to concern more highly skilled workers and the propensity to generate rapid employment growth in this sector is constrained by incomes (and demand) in the rest of the economy (Rodrik, 2015$_{[16]}$).

With the creation of more productive jobs, average earnings have increased. However, there are large differences in access to technology across countries and the many small informal firms in Asia and the Pacific often do not have the capacity and incentives to invest in technology. In the Asia/Pacific region the informal sector is large and the majority of workers remain in low-paid low-productivity jobs. This curtails the prospects for such rapid service-led growth and also raises important concerns around widening earnings and income inequality and increased labour market polarisation, as for example, in India (OECD, 2017[17]).

In both Asia/Pacific countries as well as the OECD, there are growing concerns about the possible negative employment effects of continued digitalisation (ADB, 2018[2]; OECD, 2018[18]), and its implications for social protection (OECD, 2018[19]). Technological progress can displace some manual and routine jobs, but often automation concerns some tasks of a job, in which case automation can change the nature of a job and the tasks involved, and "free up" the worker to focus on more complex or new tasks involved in the job. Nevertheless, the dynamism embedded in rapidly evolving technological progress raises concerns that further automation could cause widespread job loss, reduce wage growth, curtail social protection coverage and widen income inequality.

A strategy for quality jobs and inclusive growth

Globalisation, digitalisation, demographic shifts and climate change are transforming the way economies work, providing new opportunities for growth, but also raising the risk of deeper inequalities if the gains from growth are not evenly shared among people, firms and regions. The focus on stronger productivity growth is necessary, but not sufficient to sustain economic growth over the long-term unless policy design effectively addresses equity issues. The opportunities for growth could be better leveraged through policies that promote broad-based growth that is beneficial to all (Pathways for Prosperity Commission, 2018[20]). Such policies include increased investment in education, in particular investing in skills of children from low-income families, promoting lifelong learning, including reskilling and upskilling displaced workers, and active labour market programmes to match unemployed workers with new job opportunities.

A well-functioning labour market is key to achieving inclusive growth and rising levels of well-being (OECD, 2018[21]). It promotes prosperity by matching workers to productive and rewarding jobs and the functioning of the labour market facilitating the adoption of new technologies and new ways of organising work by providing workers with opportunities to acquire and update relevant skills in a rapidly changing economic environment. A well-functioning labour market further ensures that increased prosperity involves increased well-being and job quality, in both monetary and non-monetary terms, by creating good job opportunities for all, including through facilitating the transition of workers and (small, often one-person) enterprises from the informal to the formal economy, ensuring that productivity gains are transmitted to wages whilst protecting and improving the living standards of the most vulnerable.

Job quality and labour market inclusiveness are an integral part of new OECD Jobs Strategy (Box 2.2). Job quality is an inherently multi-dimensional concept that refers to those job characteristics that contribute to the well-being of workers and the OECD Job Quality Framework is structured around three dimensions that are closely related to people's employment situation: earnings quality, labour market security and quality of the working environment (OECD, 2014[22]). OECD (2015[23]) further developed this framework and adapted it to emerging economies in view of the prevailing data limitations and their labour market characteristics, in particular, the weaknesses of their social protections (inadequacy of benefits and/or limited coverage of social insurance schemes), and the high incidences of informality and working poverty.

Box 2.2. **The new OECD Jobs Strategy (2018)**

The new OECD Jobs Strategy launched in 2018 (OECD, 2018[24]) affirms the links between strong and sustained economic growth and the quantity of jobs, but also recognizes job quality as well as labour market inclusiveness as central policy priorities. The key policy recommendations of the new OECD Jobs strategy are organised around three broad principles: i) Promoting an environment in which high-quality jobs can flourish; ii) Preventing labour market exclusion and protecting individuals against labour market risks; and, iii) Preparing for future opportunities and challenges in a rapidly changing economy and labour market.

In comparison to previous strategies the framework of the new OECD Jobs Strategy has been broadened and now encompasses three over-arching policy objectives that together define good labour market performance and are each necessary for inclusive growth and well-being more generally (OECD, 2018[24]):

- *More and better jobs*. This captures the labour market situation in terms of both the quantity of jobs (e.g. unemployment, labour force participation, working time) as well the quality of jobs by taking account of the three dimensions of the OECD Job Quality Framework that are key for worker's well-being: i) earnings; ii) labour market security; and iii) the quality of the work environment (OECD, 2014[22]). OECD (2015[23]) extended this framework for emerging economies by using the incidence of very long working hours as a proxy measure of the quality of the work environment.
- *Labour market inclusiveness*. This dimension focuses on the distribution of opportunities and outcomes across individuals. Ensuring equal opportunities to succeed in the labour market for all reduces the risk that people are excluded from fully participating in the labour market and fall into poverty. Labour market inclusiveness therefore relates to both dynamic aspects of inequality such as the prospects for social mobility and career advancement, as well as static ones such as the distribution of individual earnings and household incomes, and differences in access to quality jobs between different socio-economic groups.
- *Adaptability and resilience*. This dimension relates to the effectiveness with which individuals, institutions and societies absorb, adapt to, and make the most out of shocks and new opportunities, which arise as a result of economic crises and megatrends (e.g. technological change, including automation and digitalisation, climate and demographic change and globalisation).

Outcomes along these dimensions of labour market performance do not depend on labour market policies alone but also on a range of other policies, including sound macroeconomic and financial policies, productivity-enhancing policies in product, financial, and housing markets, tax policies, entrepreneurship policies, regional policies, as well as the protection of property rights and the rule of law. In turn, labour market policies do not only affect labour market performance but also other dimensions of economic performance, well-being and social progress. Thus, a whole-of-government approach is needed to ensure the effective implementation of any jobs strategy that is an integral part of a policy framework for inclusive growth (OECD, 2018[21]).

Informal employment is widespread in Asia and the Pacific

High and persistent informal employment (Box 2.3) is a major policy concern, which complicates the challenge of promoting strong productivity growth and more inclusive labour markets (OECD, 2018[25]). Informality is associated with low productivity as many informal firms are over-represented in the bottom part of the productivity distribution. Informal workers are often not covered by social protection arrangements or collective labour agreements, and with limited mobility between formal and informal sectors, informality is often tantamount to persistent lack of labour market inclusiveness. As informal firms and workers often pay no or limited taxes, the size of the informal sector limits the tax base and the redistributive nature of national tax/benefit systems.

Box 2.3. **Informal employment, the informal sector and the informal economy**

The term ***informal economy*** encompasses all economic activities by workers or economic units that are – in law or practice – not covered or insufficiently covered by formal arrangements. The definition of ***informal employment*** is based on jobs as observation units and the characteristics of the employment relationship and status in employment. Employees are considered to have informal jobs if their employment relationship is not subject to labour regulation, taxation, social protection or entitlement to certain employment benefits (advance notice of dismissal, paid annual or sick leave, etc.). Informality in employment-relationships can concern non-declaration or partial declaration of jobs and earnings (to remain below certain thresholds over which (more) income tax and social security contributions are due), and frequently concerns casual jobs of short-duration, and jobs that involve limited hours per day. However, it also concerns many full-time workers and informal own-account workers who are sub-contracted by companies rather than being hired on basis of a formal employment contract.

All contributing (unpaid) family workers are considered to have informal jobs. Activities of persons engaged in the production of goods for own final use are also considered informal jobs.

Employers and own-account workers are considered to have an informal job when their company (production unit) is informal. ***Informal sector enterprises*** are private unincorporated enterprises which are not registered under specific forms of national legislation, such as factories or commercial acts, tax or social security laws, professional groups' regulatory acts, or similar acts, laws or regulations established by national legislative bodies and/or whose employees are not registered. The ***informal sector*** concerns the outputs of goods and services generated by unregistered and unincorporated enterprises or own-account workers that do not have a complete set of accounts and/or are not registered under national legislation.

For a discussion of methodological concepts and measurement issues regarding informal employment, see (Chen, 2012[26]; Hussmanns, 2004[27]; OECD, 2015[23]; ILO, 2018[28]).

There are strong links between informality and poverty (Jütting and De Laiglesia, 2009[29]). Workers in informal employment are more likely to be poor than workers in formal employment, either because they earn lower incomes or because, they share their income with a high number of economic dependents within the household (ILO, 2016[30]). Informality and poverty have important consequences which include the limited capacity of individuals or low-profit firms to adopt a long-term perspective rather than short-term coping strategies, to raise their productivity and to afford the cost of formalisation.

Although difficult to measure by its very nature, the share of informal employment – those workers who are not covered by social protection through their employment contract, is high in emerging economies (OECD, 2018[25]) and is estimated to concern about

60% of total employment around the world (ILO, 2018[28]). It is deemed most common in Africa at over 85% of all employment, but informal employment is widespread in the Asian Pacific region too: the share of informal employment in total employment is high at 68.2% while for employment in the non-agricultural sector this is somewhat lower at 59.2% (ILO, 2018[28]). In other words, the majority of the workers in Asia and the Pacific are in jobs that do not entitle them to social and health supports.

The prevalence of informal employment varies across countries and economic sectors. To start with the latter, almost all workers in the agricultural sector in the Asia/ Pacific region are considered to be in informal employment, compared to almost 70% of employment in industry and just over 50% of service sector employment (ILO, 2018[28]). The size of the (subsistence) agricultural sector is one of the key drivers of variation in the prevalence of informal employment across countries. This helps to explain why the share of informal employment in employment is below 20% in an industrialised OECD such a Japan, less than one-third in Brunei Darussalam and Korea, two/thirds or more in relative poor counties (*see Indicator 3.1, GDP per capita*) and over 90% of all employment in Cambodia, Lao PDR and Nepal (Figure 2.5).

Figure 2.5. **Informal employment concerns over two/thirds of workers in Asia and the Pacific**

The share of informal employment in total employment, 2016 or latest available

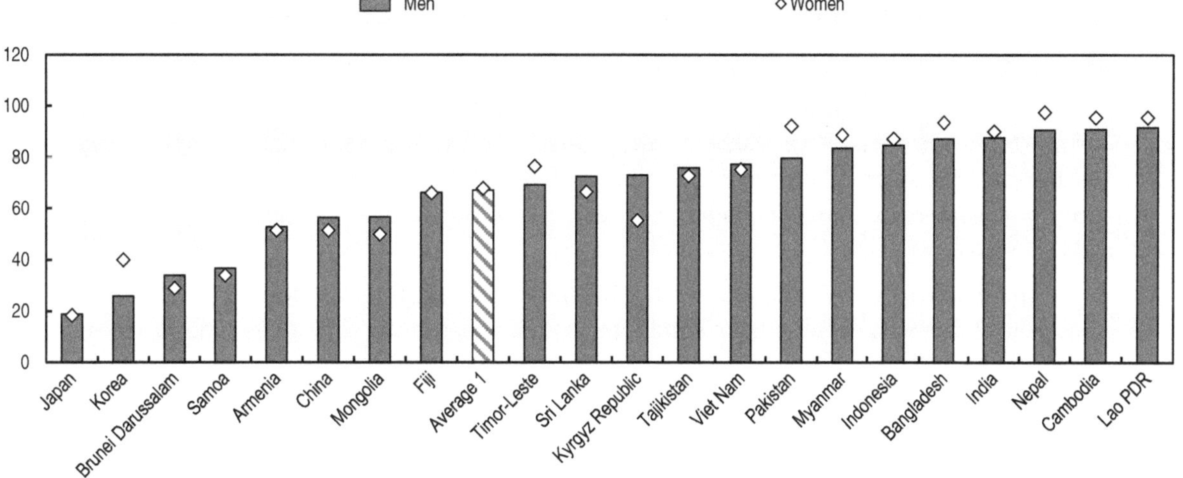

1. Average for the countries included in the Figure.

Note: Data are for 2016 for Indonesia and Fiji; 2015 for Armenia, Mongolia, Myanmar, Pakistan and Viet Nam; 2014 for Brunei Darussalam and Korea; 2013 for Bangladesh, China, the Kyrgyz Republic, Sri Lanka and Timor-Leste; 2012 for Cambodia, India and Samoa; 2010 for Japan and Lao PDR; 2009 for Tajikistan and 2008 for Nepal, see Annex A2 of ILO (2018).

Source: ILO (2018), *Women and men in the informal economy: a statistical picture – third edition*, and the Employment and Unemployment Survey for Fiji.

StatLink http://dx.doi.org/10.1787/888933899660

Overall, the incidence of informal employment does not vary much by gender. Female (67.3%) and male workers (68.0%) appear to be equally likely to engage in informal employment across Asia and the Pacific (Figure 2.5). However, an important difference is that women are much more likely than men to be in the most vulnerable segments of the informal economy as domestic workers, as home-based workers in the lower tiers of global supply chains or as contributing family workers, usually considered as unpaid. Women are also more likely to be in employment for shorter hours. The incidence of short-working hours across Asia and the Pacific region is 10% on average, as 7.5% of male and 14.8% of female informal workers work less than 20 hours per week. All these factors contribute to persistent gender pay gaps.

More than 85% of jobs in rural areas belong to informal employment while less than half of jobs (47.4%) in urban areas are in informal employment. The high exposure of agricultural workers to informality only partially explains the urban/rural differences in informality rates. Other factors include: the institutional and economic environment with limited access to public infrastructure and services; personal and employment characteristics of the rural population (lower levels of education and under-representation of skilled jobs); and traditions and rural actors' perception of laws and regulations and social norms (Jonasson, $2012_{[31]}$; Weng, $2015_{[32]}$).

Who are the informal workers and what are their employment conditions?

Informal workers in each country have diverse personal profiles of age, sex, education levels, working hours and employment status. Understanding who informal workers are, and where they work is important to address issues around the lack of social protection for informal workers.

There seems to be an u-curve relationship between age and informality. Youth (age 15-24) and elderly workers (over 65 years of age) are most likely to be in informal employment: in both age groups, around 85% of workers are in informal employment across the Asia/ Pacific region. By comparison, about 60% of workers aged 35-54 are in informal employment (ILO, $2018_{[28]}$).

In most Asian countries, the informal economy absorbs a large share of low-skilled workers. About half of the workers in informal employment Asia and the Pacific have either no education or primary schooling at best, and this concerns two out of three informal workers in Cambodia, India, Indonesia, Myanmar, Nepal, Pakistan and Timor-Leste (ILO, $2018_{[28]}$).

There is hardly any difference in the likelihood of engaging in informal employment between those workers who have completed primary education and those who have not. However, the likelihood to be in informal employment decreases sharply – from 94.9% to 58.9% and 30.7%, for workers who have completed secondary and tertiary education, respectively. The effect of education on the probability of being in informal employment is largest for countries in East Asia for which data is available (China, Japan, Korea and Mongolia): 90% of workers without primary education are in informal employment while this is just over 10% for workers with tertiary educational attainment (ILO, $2018_{[28]}$).

The low level of educational attainment among informal workers in Asia and the Pacific is a key reason of the low productivity of the informal sector. Other factors include the lack of access to markets and key public goods and services, or limited access to credit for self-employed workers.

Most of the workers in informal employment in the region (65 to 90%) are either employees[2] or own-account workers, while the proportion of contributory family workers among informal workers tends to be largest (20 to 40%) among relatively poor countries (Figure 2.6). More than 85% of all workers in informal employment in Asia and the Pacific work in informal sector enterprises, and almost 75% of total informal employment is concentrated in small economic units of less than 10 workers (Bonnet, $2019_{[33]}$). However, there are many workers in *informal* employment in the *formal* sector, as for example in

Bangladesh, Brunei Darussalam, Cambodia, Fiji, India, Lao PDR, Timor Leste and Viet Nam (Figure 2.7). In fact, 20% of the workers who are informally employed in the formal sector are in enterprises of 50 workers and over (Bonnet, 2019[33]).

Figure 2.6. **Most informal workers are employees or own-account workers with contributory family workers most prevalent in the poorest countries**

Informal employment as share of total employment by employment status, 2016 or the latest available

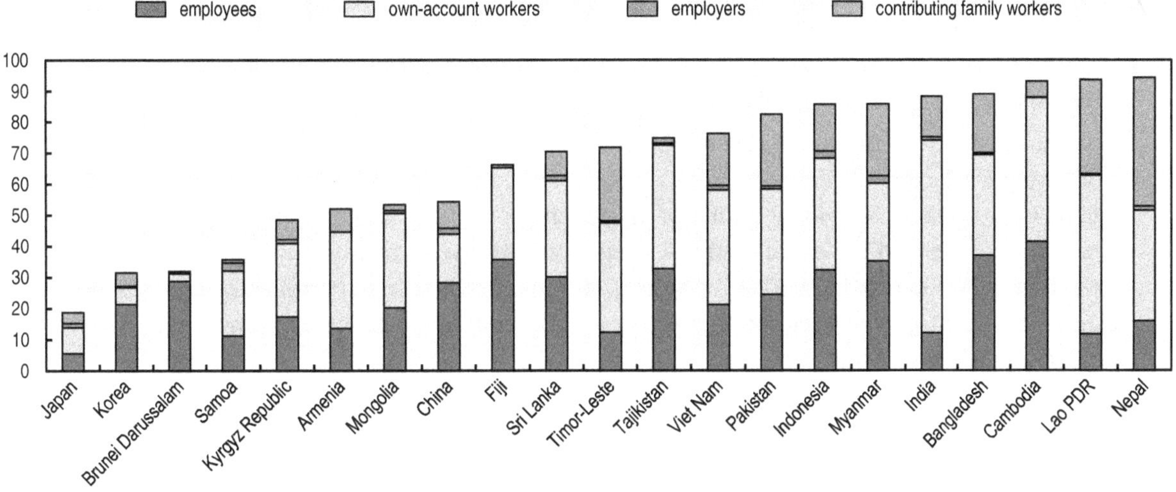

Source: ILO (2018), *Women and men in the informal economy: a statistical picture – third edition.*

StatLink http://dx.doi.org/10.1787/888933899679

Figure 2.7. **In many Asian countries, the majority of employees is in the informal sector**

Share and composition of informal wage employment (% employees), or the latest available

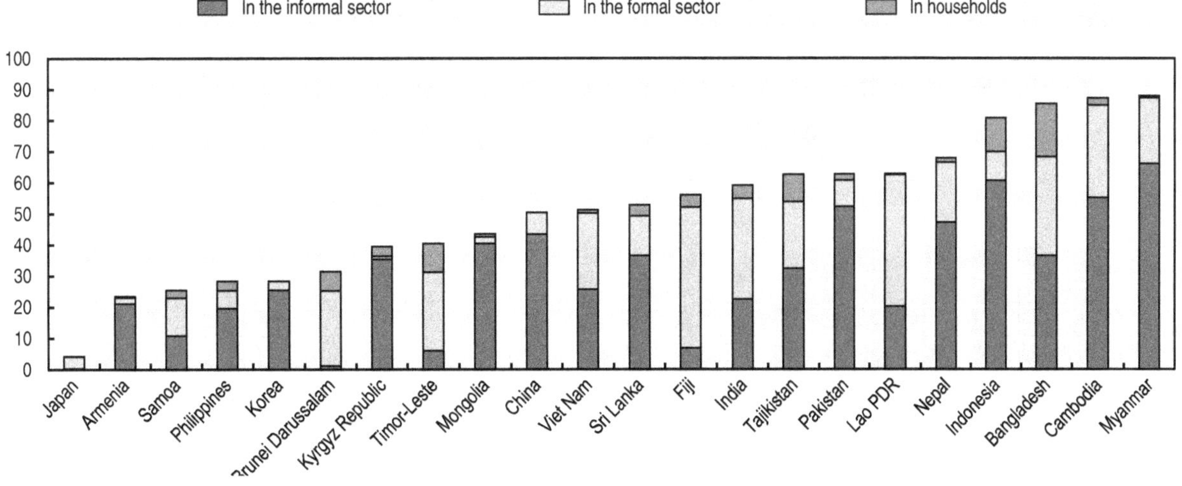

Source: ILO (2018), *Women and men in the informal economy: a statistical picture – third edition.*

StatLink http://dx.doi.org/10.1787/888933899698

These labour market outcomes have implications for the policy approach towards increasing social protection coverage among informal workers. For own account workers and self-employed workers in the informal sector increasing social protection coverage is linked to formalization of the economic unit in which they are working. This may be promoted for example by financial incentives for registration and straightforward procedures for contributions and benefit delivery by digital means (OECD, 2012). The formalization of informal sector enterprises is also a pre-condition for the formalization of the employment relationship of employees working in these sector enterprises. The formal recognition of the employment relationships as well as improved monitoring and enforcement of labour standards could contribute to increasing social protection coverage among informal employees working in the formal sector and among own-account workers whose employment relationship is disguised through sub-contracting by formal sector enterprises (Bonnet, 2019).

The quality of informal employment

In addition to not being covered by social protection arrangements, the length of the working week can be taken as a proxy for the quality of the working environment (Box 2.3). This is by no means an ideal indicator as evidence on the relationship between very long working hours and life satisfaction is mixed, but otherwise results suggest that working very long hours impairs workers' physical and mental health, particularly when workers have little control over their work schedule and the number of hours (Bassanini and Caroli, 2014[35]; OECD, 2016[36]).

Working hours suggest that job quality is low for many informal workers across the region: around one fifth of informal workers in Brunei Darussalam, China, Mongolia, and Nepal work more than 60 hours per week. Just over 40% of the informal workers work 48 hours per week or more and almost 15% of workers put in more than 60 hours per week (Figure 2.8). This is 35% and 12%, respectively, for employees in formal employees, who also frequently work long hours. Gender gaps in working hours exists across Asia and the Pacific, 15.4% of male and 11.7% of female informal workers – work more than 60 hours per week (ILO, 2018[28]).

Figure 2.8. **Informal workers often put in very long hours.**

Percentage of those in informal employment who work more that 48 or 60 hours per week, 2016 or the latest

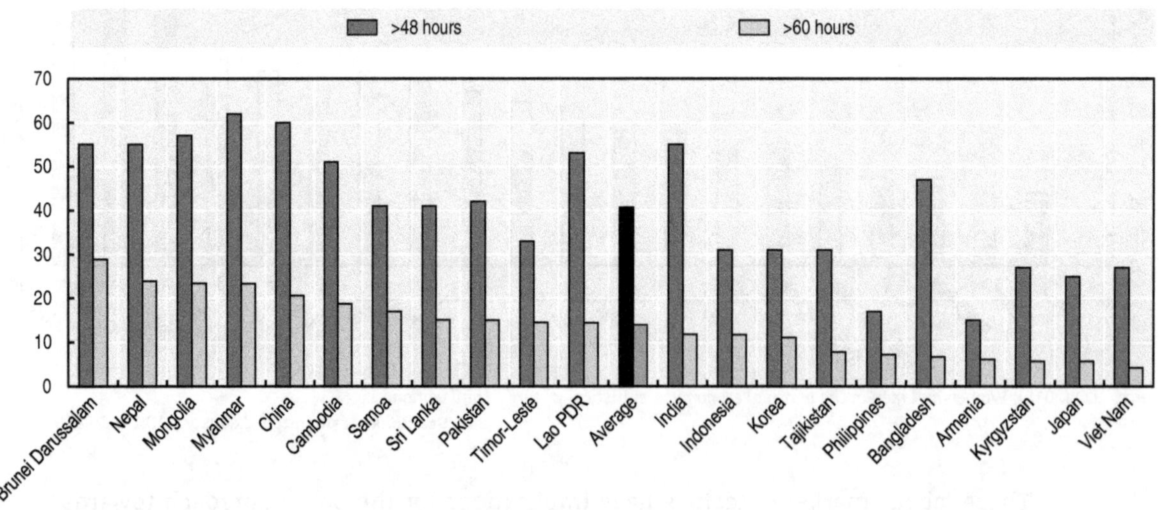

Note: For years see the note to Figure 2.5.

Source: ILO (2018), *Women and men in the informal economy: a statistical picture – third edition.*

StatLink http://dx.doi.org/10.1787/888933899717

The future of Social Protection in Asia and the Pacific

Social protection (Box 2.1) encompasses a wide range of public and private programmes to protect individuals and their families from predictable life course risks (dependency in childhood, retirement from work, frailty in old age) as well as the unpredictable risks that individuals and their families face during their years of working age (sickness, temporary or long-term disability or other health conditions, accidents at work, personal job loss and general increases in unemployment in recessions, irregular work, and family breakdown). These risks are generally associated with falls in household income and or increased (health-related) expenses and social protection programmes are designed to partly compensate for these income losses and provide services and care that enable people to return to work or other productive activities.

Changes in the nature of work and labour markets potentially pose new challenges to the social protection systems of high-income countries, particularly those relying on contributory social insurance systems. As temporary work and changing forms of employment contracts become more prevalent, the assumption of full-time, permanent formal employment threatens to become less common, potentially undermining welfare state finances as well as the social protection of workers and their families (OECD, 2018[19]).

Changes in the nature of work will also challenge the extension of social insurance in middle and low-income countries in Asia and the Pacific. However, as discussed above, the majority of workers in Asia and the Pacific are already excluded from social protection support. Technological change and new work forms, will merely add to the already huge challenge of extending social protection coverage among existing workers in the region.

Non-contributory systems – such as Australia (Box 2.4) and New Zealand – can also face important challenges, even if they do not require explicit contributions to secure eligibility for coverage of social risks. Social spending does require appropriate levels of taxation in order to be financed. To the extent that changes in future work patterns undermine adequate revenue collection, social protection may be put at risk. A further factor is that the administration of income-testing becomes much more complicated if patterns of work become irregular or other circumstances, such as multiple job holding become common.

Box 2.4. **Social protection and safeguarding minimum employment conditions in Australia**

The Australian social security system differs from the social insurance systems common in other OECD countries. In Australia, most government benefits are flat-rate entitlements financed from general government revenue, and there are no explicit social security contributions required as a condition of eligibility. Most benefits are income tested and asset tested, so that entitlements reduce as resources increase (Whiteford, 2017[37]). Within these income and assets tests, income from self-employment and business resources are treated differently from other employment or unearned income. To a large degree, payments are the responsibility of the Commonwealth (national) government, with eligibility conditions and entitlements being uniform across the country.

There are programmes at the level of Australian state governments – notably compensation for work accidents and motor vehicle accidents – that involve contributions of different sorts and in the case of compensation for accidents or illness arising from work also pay high wage replacement rates. In addition, many public sector employees and some private sector workers also are covered by defined-benefit occupational pension

Box 2.4. **Social protection and safeguarding minimum employment conditions in Australia** *(cont.)*

schemes for retirement (most of these are now closed to new entrants). Since the early 1990s, there has also been a mandatory private pension system – the Superannuation Guarantee – covering most employees, which requires employers to contribute to individual accounts for their employees (currently 9.5%). These can be supplemented by employee contributions, which are supported by extensive tax concessions.

The Australian government income support system is not contributory, and coverage of the population is broad. The main criteria for being covered are: meeting residence requirements; falling into specific eligibility categories; and, satisfying income- and asset tests. Duration of payment is not time limited, with income support payments being paid indefinitely subject to the continued meeting of eligibility criteria. Benefits are legal entitlements and recipients can appeal to administrative and judicial tribunals in case of disagreements about administrative decisions.

Access to the healthcare system and government reimbursement of health-care fees is also based on residence rather than contributions, even though the healthcare system is partly financed by a levy in addition to income tax.

As a result of these design features, formal employment is not required as a condition for receiving social security payments. However, workers may also be entitled to various forms of social protection as part of their employment package.

Australia's statutory minimum wage is the third highest in the OECD in purchasing power terms (OECD Employment Database), and due to the relatively low level of taxes and social security contributions paid by low-income earners (OECD, 2015[38]), the purchasing power of the full-time, after-tax minimum wage is the highest in the OECD (OECD, 2015[39]).

The scope of workplace regulation of pay and conditions has changed significantly over time. The past 30 years or so have witnessed radical changes, with the decentralisation and individualisation of what was "a relatively centralised framework of wages [and conditions] determination" (Wright and Lansbury, 2016[40]). These changes have enabled workplace-level collective negotiation of pay and conditions (agreement is contained in enforceable enterprise agreements) whilst retaining industry/occupation specific legal minima (called "modern awards") which enterprise agreements may diverge from if they leave employees better off overall. Modern awards set minimum wages as well as other working conditions such as overtime payments and leave conditions and the overall contents are specified in the Fair Work Act (FWA) of 2009, Australia's principal employment rights statute.

Apart from high income-replacement – up to full-replacement – rates for accidents at work, a majority of employed people are entitled to paid sick leave and paid carers' leave of up to ten days a year (combined) paid at full wage levels, as well as paid annual and public holidays. Higher rates of wages are payable at for work at weekends and on public holidays. There is a significant group of workers – known as "casuals" in Australia – who are not entitled to paid sick leave or paid holidays, but who are entitled to a higher rate of hourly pay (about 20% higher) to compensate them for the lack of paid leave. The self-employed are not covered by these provisions, and it is therefore financially rewarding for employers if they are able to define employees as self-employed or independent contractors.

Many of the conditions attached to employment do require enforcement, and at the Commonwealth level there are two key agencies:

1. The Fair Work Commission (FWC) is an independent tribunal responsible for maintaining a safety net of minimum wages and employment conditions (Australian Government, 2018[41]).

Box 2.4. **Social protection and safeguarding minimum employment conditions in Australia** *(cont.)*

The Commission sets national minimum wages annually, following consideration of submissions made by employer organization, unions and government. The FWC also reviews and sets each "modern award". Neither modern awards nor enterprise agreements may undercut a yet more limited set of minimum employment conditions contained in the Fair Work Act (Stewart et al., 2016[42]).

2. The Fair Work Ombudsman (FWO) is also an independent agency which enforces compliance with the Fair Work Act 2009 and they also provide advice and education services to employers and employees (Australian Government, 2018[43]). Most breaches of the Act involve civil remedies and can be punished by fines, while some breaches can be criminal offences (e.g. bribery). The FWO is concerned with individual cases of disregard for the law, exploitation of vulnerable workers and complex supply chains or networks where there is a risk of employees being classified as self-employed and therefore not covered by the conditions described above. The FWO can also initiate wider inquiries, e.g. on the procurement of security services by local governments, and reports of these inquiries are publicly available. In 2016-17 the FWO issued 665 infringement notices, 192 compliance notices, 40 enforceable undertakings and initiated 55 civil penalty litigations (Australian Government, 2018[43]).

The challenge of automation

There are widespread concerns about the possible job-losses economies might incur with continued digitalisation. Using advances in Machine Learning (ML) and Mobile Robotics (MR) to categorise occupations according to their susceptibility to computerisation, Frey and Osborne (2013[44]) estimated that about 47% of total US employment is "at risk" of becoming automated over the next one to two decades. This involves mainly routine intensive jobs – in transportation, logistics, the bulk of office and administrative support workers and labour in production. They also conclude that jobs with high wages and requiring high educational attainment are less at risk.

Arntz, Gregory and Zierahn (2016[45]) use a task-based rather than occupation-based approach to estimating the effect of automation. They found that in 21 OECD countries 9% of jobs are at risk of automation, with high-skill and high-paid jobs more likely to be secure.[3] More recent evidence for 32 OECD countries suggests that at the current state of technology 14% of jobs on average across the OECD have a high risk of automation while another 32% of jobs may experience significant change to the manner in which they are carried out (OECD, 2018[18]), with large variance in "automatability" across countries (Nedelkoska and Quintini, 2018[46]).

In some economies in developing Asia, about half of the jobs could be affected by automation: some may disappear altogether while many others will be transformed (ADB, 2018[2]). However, there are a large number of workers in the region who are in the informal sector often in low-productivity jobs. While technically many jobs are "automatable" in emerging economies, it may not be economically attractive to do so because of several factors including relatively low wages and high costs of investment in ICT. So, while there is a risk of job-loss there is also an important risk of increasing labour market and economic inequality.

The projected impact of changes in technology on future work patterns may well be similar to the past impact of "skills-biased technological change" (Card and Dinardo, 2002[47]).

While technological change is certainly not the only factor behind widening wage inequalities in high income countries, it is commonly argued that it can be associated with labour market polarisation, where middle skill jobs are lost and there is a growth in both high-skill and low skill jobs, potentially leading to a hollowing-out of the middle.

The skills and education gradient in the impact of automation projected by (Frey and Osborne, 2013[44]) and also found by (Arntz, Gregory and Zierahn, 2016[45]) suggests that even if the majority of jobs do not disappear, there is the possibility of further labour market polarisation in the future. The response to this challenge is to increase investment in education and training in order to develop the appropriate skills for jobs complementing the new technology (OECD, 2018[48]). A better understanding, valuing and rewarding of skills seen as traditionally female (such as care work) could also lead to reclassifying many jobs into higher skills levels and improve economic well-being.

Digital labour markets

With the growing number of digital platforms, two distinct types of jobs and labour markets can be identified (Pesole et al., 2018[49]). The first type of digital labour market can be categorised as electronically transmittable services, or **Online Labour Markets (OLMs)**. Examples include Amazon Mechanical Turk (Limer, 2014[50]), Upwork and Freelancers. These platforms enable work to be requested and provided anywhere in the world and include, for example, the design of websites, advertising campaigns, proof-reading, editing, writing student essays or even following people on Twitter, completing Facebook surveys or loading videos to YouTube.

Offshore call centres are analogous services, even if not necessarily digital. The fact that these jobs can be performed anywhere in the world and delivered via the Internet is seen as creating a "flat world", where people in low income countries – with the appropriate skills – can compete with more highly paid individuals in high-income countries. As well as providing cheaper services than may be available from workers in high-income countries – subject to differences in the quality of the service – employers may benefit from time differences (delivery of services overnight, rather than by the end of their own next working day). In all, there are potential gains for emerging economies in Asia and the Pacific both from digital platforms and also from technological change, particularly in terms of promoting access to social services through online tools (Box 2.5).

The second type of digital labour market also involves digital matching of clients and providers of services, but service-delivery is physical. Pesole et al. (2018[49]) describes these as **mobile labour markets (MLMs)**, and examples of these include Deliveroo, Uber, and Lyft. Delivery of food or taxi services, for example, by definition means that the service provider has to be in the same city or town as the purchaser (Box 2.6). While digital platforms sometimes claim that there are very significant number of people employed in providing these services, Pesole et al (2018[49]), suggest that they involve no more than 1 or 2% of the labour force in the United Kingdom and the United States.

The platform labour market is, however, a subset of what is often called the "gig economy". For example, in the United States it has been estimated that more than a quarter of workers participate in the gig economy in some capacity (ILR School and Future of Work Initiative, 2018[64]), either as their primary income source or as a supplementary source of income. Katz and Krueger (2016[65]) estimated that 15.8% of the American labour force are engaged in independent work as their main job, where this includes temporary,

Box 2.5. **Aadhaar: the use of biometric smartcards in social service delivery in India**

Further increasing access to social protection is an imperative for achieving more inclusive and cohesive societies in the Asia/Pacific region. The challenge facing many economies with a large rural sector or a large urban informal economy is overcoming administrative bottlenecks limiting coverage extension of social protection, not least because of the very limited capacity to register participants in insurance schemes and/or collect contributions from employers and employees. New technologies can represent a great opportunity for governments in the region to track social protection eligibility, to adapt or simplify registration and benefit-award procedures, improved access to information and generally help extend coverage to all those who need social support.

One approach worth considering is India's effort of equipping all its citizens with a digital identity. This initiative, known as "Aadhaar", already covers more than a billion Indians, and those who enrolled in Aadhaar received a unique 12-digit identification number after submitting their fingerprints and retina scans. This large biometric identity database covers welfare and tax payments and access to social services, as for example, making payments to low-income households that are eligible for the "cooking gas subsidy" and "social assistance pensions". Aadhaar can also be used for financial services, such as daily bank transfers, but in a landmark ruling the Indian Constitutional court limited the scope of the Aadhaar scheme, saying it could not be compulsory for bank accounts, mobile connections or school admissions (BBC, 2018[51]).

In a comprehensive RCT-based evaluation of Aadhaar (Muralidharan, Niehaus and Sukhtankar, 2016[52]; 2017[53]) evaluate the impact of the smartcards on beneficiaries of the National Rural Employment Guarantee Scheme (NREGS), the Public Distributions system (the National Food Security Act), and the social assistance pensions (SSP). In the state Andhra Pradesh, Aadhaar made it more difficult for programme staffers to over-report the number of clients and siphon off programme-funds and leakage of this type reduced by 41%, similarly Aadhaar reduced leakage of this type with respect to the SSP pensions programme. However, while Aadhaar may help address identity fraud, by its nature it is more difficult for Aadhaar to address "quantity fraud" when beneficiaries receive only a fraction of their entitlement as with the PDS programme (Banerjee, 2016) The Aadhaar experience can be further improved. For example, the regular and independent collection of representative data on programme access and exclusion error could help identify the share of legally entitled benefits that eligible beneficiaries are receiving. Aadhaar could also enhance customer choice in terms of the form of support (cash or in-kind) and portability across ration shops of PDS distributors.

on call, contracting and freelance work. The "gig economy" data link above also states that only about 1% of the US workforce regularly use online digital platforms to connect with work opportunities, so currently digital labour markets are a relatively small sub-set of the gig economy. It is usually considered that a much greater number of jobs in emerging economies are of this type.

While digital platform jobs are the product of technological innovation, like other "gig economy" jobs, the challenges they raise for the future labour market are regulatory. Some of this work is essentially piece-work. These developments are related to outsourcing (of tasks) and offshoring and reflect changes in the nature of firms. This type of work blurs distinctions between employees and self-employed. Many may involve regulatory "arbitrage" – where the company is able to provide cheaper services because it seeks to avoid to varying degrees the licensing requirements, as well as tax liabilities and employee

Box 2.6. **Employment Accident insurance for drivers of on-line taxi services**

Recent years have seen a rapid expansion of the on-line taxi service market, with most 20% of the world population using such services at least once during 2015/16 (Holmes, 2017[55]; Marciano, 2016[56]). Overall revenue of the market was estimated to be around USD 36 billion in 2016 and may increase eightfold by 2030 (Burgstaller et al., 2017[57]). On-line taxi services play an important role in the emerging economies in South Asia. For example, in Indonesia, where motorbikes are more frequently used than vehicles for taxi-services, the market is estimated to grow from USD 800 million in 2015 to USD 5.6 billion in 2025 (Purnell, 2016[58]).

The GO-JEK company in Indonesia engages in "on-line" service provision including food delivery, courier and domestic cleaning services (Ford and Honan, 2017[59]). In 2011, GO-JEK started its motorbike taxi booking service with a call centre and 20 drivers in; but in 2018 it had about 1 million drivers: these are not employees, but individual "partners" who are self-employed and/or informal workers, without social protection or labour market regulation coverage. GO-JEK drivers – with a registered motorbike can engage in a partnership contract with the GO-JEK company, and receive courses about health and safety. Road safety is a major concerns in emerging economies; traffic accidents caused 38 297 fatalities in Indonesia in 2013 (WHO Global Health Observatory, 2018[60]). Since 2015, GO-JEK provides accident insurance for its partner drivers and passengers. It also provides health insurance to its drives and their families on a voluntary basis (Prabowo, 2018[61]).

In Malaysia, concerns about road safety – about 7 000 fatalities or 23 per 100 000 people (Department Statistics of Malaysia, 2015[62]), contributed to the development of "the Self-Employment Social Security Act" in 2017. This Act stipulates that taxi drivers, of which there are about 83 000 conventional taxi-drivers and "on-line" taxi service drivers from Grab and Uber, have to register with the Employment Injury Scheme. Failure to do so is a legal offense which fines up to RM 10 000 (USD 2 577) and/or two years imprisonment.

Registered drivers can choose their insurance scheme from four options depending on insurable income, renewable every year (Social Security Organisation of Malaysia, 2018[63]). This scheme provides eight different cash and in-kind benefits to insured taxi drivers and their families: medical benefits, free medical treatment of employment injuries or occupational diseases; temporary disability benefit for medically certified periods of leave; permanent disability benefit, up to 90% of estimated insured earnings; attendance allowances for carers of a permanently disabled person (USD 128.87 per month); survivor benefits; funeral benefits; physical or vocational rehabilitation supports; and, education benefits. As June 2018 about 7 000 out of 83 000 drivers had registered with the scheme.

on-costs. Indeed, informality also concerns many of the new jobs that are emerging in the wake of technological change, digitalization, outsourcing and subcontracting, and many of the on-line platform workers face similar challenges in terms of income security, employment conditions and recourse in case of unfair treatment as informal workers in more traditional economic sectors (Berg, 2016[66]; ILO, 2018[67]).

The risks of these types of jobs are that they pay less than the minimum wage (reduced further by the fees charged by the digital platform), and provide no workers compensation or sick leave or superannuation. The maintenance of occupational health and safety standards may also be a concern.

In terms of social protection, as with other informal workers, obvious questions are whether income tax or social insurance contributions where relevant are paid, and whether VAT payments are made. Similarly, many of the relatively low paid tasks advertised on these platforms raise the question of whether the earnings have been declared for social security income tests, where relevant. The evidence suggests that total employment derived from these platforms is a relatively small at present, but to the extent that they grow in future, they will potentially have an impact across a wide range of areas of social protection.

Social protection challenges

There is a very fundamental issue to be considered before deciding whether further reforms are needed to social security arrangements. That is whether it is desirable to adjust the benefit system to deal with irregular work[4] or whether the prevalence of irregular work should be limited through regulation of working conditions – or what is the best middle ground between these approaches.

There is also a link between the adequacy of wages and working conditions and the level of the social security safety net. Reforming a well-developed social security system as in OECD countries to deal with greater instability in working hours or to support temporary workers in times when they are between contracts can be regarded as supporting risk-shifting from employers to government and taxpayers. Should government and workers fill the financial gap that is left by reduced employer contributions for workers who are now working on their own account (OECD, 2018$_{[19]}$)?

In many ways this challenge is similar to the existing policy conundrum on informality. How can existing informal relationships be recognized so that they provide access to social security benefits? How can coverage for (independent) informal workers and their families be extended through existing schemes? Can policy help by extending coverage to low-income groups by partially or fully covering contributions though government subsidies (see, for example the discussion on experiences in Indonesia and Korea below)?

Extending social insurance has direct effects on formalization, the extension of social assistance programmes has not, even though it can be considered as an enabling condition providing more stable and predictable income to workers in the informal economy. In any case, social assistance programmes matter (see, for example Box 2.7. The Benazir Income Support Programme (BISP) in Pakistan): they reduce the poverty gap/headcount and income inequality. Then again, payment rates are often low and many gaps in coverage remain, particularly in low-income countries (World Bank Group, 2018$_{[68]}$). Nevertheless, together with other policies to improve productivity, social assistance programmes could help create in the long run, the necessary conditions for a formalization of employment relationships and amalgamation with social insurance schemes with higher payment rates.

It is widely argued that if the level of benefits in the income support system is too high, then this may give incentives for individuals to reduce their work effort. The logical extension of this is that if the level of benefits are too low or the conditions to satisfy eligibility are too onerous, then workers will put up with unsatisfactory work conditions because the alternative of claiming benefits while looking for a better job is unacceptable. Just as it is difficult to justify adequate social security benefits without an adequate minimum wage, the maintenance of an adequate minimum wage and working conditions also requires an adequate benefit safety net.

There are other major challenges to social protection than those arising from changing work patterns. Population ageing is affecting many countries, particularly in North East Asia, where rapid increases in life expectancy and even more rapid declines in fertility have resulted in the fastest rates of population ageing in history (*see Indicator 3.5, Old-age support ratio*).

The speed of change can provide challenges in its own right, partly to the extent that it is associated with social changes such as increases in family breakdown and the weakening of traditional family ties. A further factor is that rapid income and wage growth can mean wide gaps emerge between the retired and those working in the newer and more prosperous economy. Related to this are widening income and wealth inequalities in rapidly growing economies, as some areas of the country or some social groups do not share in the increased prosperity of those who prosper as a result of economic growth.

Population ageing and its associated implications for health care and age care will also affect the types of jobs that will be needed in the future. It is projected that the fastest growing area of employment will be "health care and social assistance", comprising both some of the highest paid and the lowest paid occupations, a factor that may further contribute to a polarised labour force.

Another area where challenges to existing systems of social protection may be growing is in relation to international migration and temporary migrant workers. In addition, to contributions and income-testing, one of the most important criteria for eligibility to various forms of social protection is citizenship or permanent residence. Migrants may have limited access to social security and health care. International evidence attests to their vulnerability to exploitation through employer evasion of work standards.

Options for social security protection

Table 2.1 shows the spectrum of income maintenance programmes ranging from conditional cash transfers, other tightly income-tested social assistance schemes, through Negative Income Taxes, demogrants, pilot schemes of Basic Income programmes (OECD, 2017[69]) – none of which actually exist on a national basis (see note to Table 2.1) – earnings-

Table 2.1. **A spectrum of possible income maintenance programmes**

Type of programme	Examples	Coverage/Eligibility
Conditional cash transfers	Brazil, Mexico, Indonesia, the Philippines	Income-tested, conditional on behaviour (school attendance, immunization)
Social Assistance	Most OECD countries, China Special Benefit – Australia	Citizens/residents; Income and assets-tested
Refundable Tax Credit	Canada GST/HST Tax Credit United States EITC	Citizens, taxpayers; May be income-tested
Negative Income Tax	Categorical – Australia General – UK Universal Credit	Citizens/residents; Income-tested
Demogrant[1]	New Zealand Superannuation Child benefits Alaska Fund Dividend	Age group/citizens State/residents
Universal Basic Income[2]	Pilot programmes, such as in Finland or the Netherlands, but no national schemes	Citizenship
Social insurance schemes, including old-age, disability and survivor pensions, and unemployment benefits	The vast majority of OECD countries, but also e.g. the notionally defined pension scheme in China	Contributions
Mandatory Private Pensions, and mandatory sick-pay	Superannuation – Australia; continued (partial) wage payments in case of illness in Germany	Contributions; employees
Voluntary private pensions and other employer-benefits;	Occupational and company pensions, employer paid parental leave benefits (various countries)	Contributions; employees
Individual Savings Accounts	Central Provident Fund Singapore	Contributions

1. A "demogrant" is a universal (non-income-tested) payment made to specified demographic groups – for example, to the aged (e.g. pensions in Canada and New Zealand) or in respect of children (child benefits) in a number of OECD countries.
2. In recent years, there has been renewed attention to the idea of a Universal Basic Income (UBI), in part because of ongoing labour market difficulties since the Global Financial Crisis and in part in anticipation of the impact of technological change. One of the essential aspects of the concept is that a UBI would involve some degree of integration of the system of cash transfers and the income tax system.

related social insurance systems with benefits for the working age population, and public or private pension schemes.

In considering possible responses to the risks discussed above, it is important to emphasise that different forms of social security will be more relevant in different national circumstances and to different groups of informal workers. In a sense, welfare state institutions, employment structures, wage-setting institutions and the regulation of employment conditions and the structure and level of taxation are "co-produced" both historically and institutionally.

To take examples from high income countries, a programme like the Earned Income Tax Credit in the United States is required to "make work pay" under conditions where minimum wages are low and the social security contributions workers make for their retirement and disability are not progressive but reduce the meagre wages of low paid workers. In many countries of Asia and the Pacific, consideration will need to be given to programmes that are relevant to countries where there a high level of agricultural workers.

Examples of reform avenues

Public social spending in many Asia/Pacific countries is low, and a rapid expansion of social programmes is unlikely to materialise, if only because of short-term budget constraints. Given this, it is imperative that countries use the existing social policy infrastructure – e.g. existing social insurance schemes, to the extent possible and target social expenditures towards the most vulnerable is required.

Non-contributory social assistance benefits will not contribute directly to the formalization of workers in informal employment, but can make a potentially important contribution to alleviating financial hardship in emerging economies since they can be targeted at those who need them most, including informal workers. In practice, however, the effectiveness of social assistance in rolling back poverty is often limited, due to a combination of insufficient resources, resulting in benefits that are not sufficiently high to lift families out of poverty, and as well as poor targeting, due to the difficulty of means-testing in emerging economies.

Extending social insurance in China and Korea

Given rapid population ageing in many Asian countries, pension coverage – the number of people in the labour force and/or the working age population who contribute to a mandatory pension system – is a key policy issue. Many Asian countries have a long-term pension coverage problem in that less than 20% of the working age population contribute to a pension: This proportion is higher in China (28%), Malaysia (39%), Singapore (45%), Korea (54%) and Japan (75%), while across the OECD almost two/thirds of the working age population makes contributions to mandatory pension schemes (*see Indicator* 5.3, Pensions: Coverage and replacement rates). This means that many Asian citizens will not be entitled to a pension, which contributes to a high risk of old-age poverty, particularly in low-income countries.

Among Asian countries, **China** has arguably been most successful in extending pension coverage among its population. Over the past decades, China has substantially increased coverage through the development of a multi-pillar pension system that includes:

- The Civil Service and Public Service Unit (PSU) scheme for civil servants and government employees;

- The Basic Urban Workers Pension (BUWP) scheme for urban workers (Salditt, Whiteford and Adema, 2008[70]) with a coverage rate (the number of participants relative to the number of workers) that increased from 60% in 2005 to 88% in 2015 (Queisser, Reilly and Hu, 2016[71]); and,
- The Basic National Resident Pension (BNRP) scheme for those not protected by the previous two schemes which in 2015 covered 505 million people (Queisser, Reilly and Hu, 2016[71]).

In all, pension coverage of these three schemes more than doubled from 360 million in 2010 to 858 million in 2015 (Zhu and Walker, 2018[72]).

The expansion of the old-age pension system in China has been attributed to several factors including rapid economic growth, firm political will and innovations in programme design that facilitated easier access (Zhu and Walker, 2018[72]). In particular, access to the BNPR scheme was enhanced by allowing those above retirement age (60 for men 55 for women) who had not met the minimum contributory requirement of 15 years of contributions to make lump-sum contributions to obtain pension rights. In addition, those who do not have the means to make the necessary lump-sum payments, can avail of a low flat-rate benefit if their working-age child(ren) contribute(s) to the pension scheme (ILO, 2017[9]).

One of the main challenges to Korea's social policy is to overcome the sharp dichotomy in the labour market between regular workers and non-regular workers (OECD, 2000[73]; OECD, 2017[74]). Regular employees generally have long-term employment contracts, seniority based wage- and career progression, access to employer-provided fringe benefits and social insurance coverage. By contrast, non-regular workers often work on renewable one-year contracts, have limited career opportunities so that pay gaps with regular workers increase markedly with age, and they have no or limited access to employment-related fringe benefits or social insurance. Similarly, the many self-employed, as well as domestic workers and workers in small agricultural and fishery workplaces are not covered. Civil servants, military officials and teachers are also not covered by National Pension and Employment insurance but they have access to occupational pension schemes.

To help reduce this social protection coverage gap between regular and non-regular and/ or informal workers, the Korean government in 2012 initiated the "Duru Nuri Social Insurance Support Programme" to encourage low-income workers in workplaces with less than 10 employees to join pension and employment insurance by offering fiscal incentives (OECD, 2017[74]). In August 2012, 33.5% and 33.8% of workers were not covered by pension and unemployment insurance schemes respectively, and this had fallen somewhat to 31% and 28.8% workers by August 2107 (Statistics Korea, 2017[75]). However, to what extent this decline is directly related to the introduction of the Duru Nuri programme is not clear, and the debate on policies measures to extend coverage among non-regular workers is ongoing.

Social security and healthcare reform in Indonesia

While existing social protection systems in Indonesia tend to be fragmented, significant progress is being made towards provisions that are more comprehensive and with improved coverage. The progressive implementation of Law No. 40/2004, also known as the National Social Security Reform Act (SJSN) involves a very ambitious programme of reform and implementation. By 2019, the system is intended to cover the entire population of more than 250 million people.

Starting in 2014, Indonesia's government launched a project to establish a compulsory national health insurance system with the aim of making basic care available to all (including foreign residents after six months of work) under a single health care system by 2019. The scheme, Jaminan Kesehatan Nasional (JKN), was implemented by the newly-formed Healthcare Social Security Agency, Badan Penyelenggara Jaminan Sosial Kesehatan (BPJS Kesehatan).[5] The system is intended to cover all employees and residents. Under JKN, the objective is that all Indonesian citizens will be able to access a wide range of health services provided by public facilities, as well as services from a few private organisations that have opted to join the scheme as providers. JKN care aims to be comprehensive, covering treatment for everyday concerns such as flu through to open-heart surgery, dialysis and chemotherapy. Private insurance continues to play a role by providing for excess or additional coverage of services not included in JKN.

In addition, in July 2015, the Workers' Social Security Agency – BPJS Ketenagakerjaan,[6] was launched with the aim of providing universal social security for Indonesian workers. Based on the principles of social insurance and compulsory savings, the programme aims to maintain decent basic living standards when participants encounter income loss or decrease resulting from workplace injuries, old age, retirement or death. BPJS Ketenagakerjaan administers employment benefits, which include elderly care, workplace accident insurance and death insurance and pensions.

For health and medical protection there is a sliding scale of contributions ranging from RP 22 500 to RP 55 000 per month (USD 2.25 to USD 4.50). The government covers medical benefits of the poor. For social security coverage, the total contribution by the employer and the employee is projected to be around 19% of earnings.[7]

The National Social Security System is part of a broader set of antipoverty programmes and government subsidies, including social assistance programmes to assist the poorest and most vulnerable. Indonesia has implemented a series of cash transfer programs since the Asian Financial Crisis. At that time, Indonesia implemented emergency social relief programmes for the poor that were later incorporated into the so called social safety net programmes (for example, the Program Jaring Pengaman Sosial) in 1999. Subsequently, unconditional cash transfers (UCTs) (Bantuan Langsung Tunai – BLT) and conditional cash transfers (CCTs) (Program Keluarga Harapan – PKH) were introduced in 2005 and 2007, respectively.

Overall, Indonesian government debt is sustainable but additional spending on health and social assistance is limited by low revenues. Additional resources must be found through greater efficiency and the raising of tax revenue which is low in comparison with other emerging economies (OECD, 2018[76]).

Extending health insurance in India

Under a programme launched nationwide in September 2018, half a billion Indian citizens will be covered by what local media outlets have dubbed "Modicare" but whose official name means "Long Life India." The health-care plan is targeted at the poorest 40% of the Indian population.

The programme gives poor families insurance coverage for expenses up to USD 6 950 in hospitals. For primary care, the government plans to open 150 000 "health and wellness" centres, staffed by nurses, traditional medicine healers and other health workers by 2020. The cost to central and state governments is estimated to be around USD 1.6 billion (Guardian, 2018[77]).

The health plan is focused on reducing "catastrophic spending" – when families have to spend more than a quarter of their incomes on health-care costs. In poor families that usually happens when a patient is hospitalized. According to a 2010 study, more than 63 million Indians – about 3-5% of the population – fall below the poverty line every year because of health-care costs. In most states, government-funded hospitals are understaffed and ill-equipped, so many people end up paying for expensive private care. Rural households source more than a quarter of their health expenses by borrowing or selling assets.

The plan will rely on partnerships with private hospitals and will promote traditional ideas of holistic health care. Nurses and practitioners of traditional Indian medicine will take "bridge courses" to enable them to provide services that include diagnosing some cancers and tuberculosis. When diagnoses are complicated, health-care workers can video-call a doctor for advice. Government-backed awareness drives and "people movements" on health issues such as nutrition will be added to existing services.

The government will pay public and private hospitals fixed rates for treating people covered under the programme. So far, 15 000 hospitals – a mix of government and private – have applied for government certification. The government has indicated that this is only a first step toward extending affordable care. It currently spends a little over 1% of GDP on public healthcare.

The most significant challenge is implementation. Federal healthcare schemes and similar publicly-funded medical insurance schemes do not have a strong record in India. Nine of 13 studies assessing such schemes reported no reduction in out-of-pocket expenses by people covered by insurance (Prinja et al., 2017$_{[78]}$).

Non-contributory social support to the most vulnerable

Other Asia/Pacific countries may not have already put a social insurance infrastructure in place and in order to rapidly address prevailing poverty and associated health and education issues, may choose to opt for developing and upscaling of non-contributory social support programmes. There is a wide range of such social support programmes, with different possible categorisations, e.g. Barrientos (2016$_{[79]}$). In the Asia/Pacific region, such programmes include, unconditional cash and/or in-kind supports, conditional cash transfers, and labour market programmes. OECD (2018$_{[25]}$) discusses the employment and work incentives of conditional and unconditional transfers but generally finds that these programmes do not generate negative employment effects in developing countries (also see Banerjee et al., (2017$_{[80]}$)).[8]

- Unconditional cash transfers (UCT), usually targeted to poor households with older household members. Examples include the Mongolian Child Money Programme (ILO, 2016$_{[81]}$; OECD, 2017$_{[74]}$), the Benazir Income Support programme (Box 2.7), the Public Distributions System of food supports in cash or in-kind in India under the National Food Security Act (Puri, 2017$_{[82]}$) or the Chinese *Urban Di Bao* system which seeks to provide a guaranteed minimum income for all households. At peak this social assistance programme that was introduced in 1993 served 7.6 million households and 23 million people in 2009, while by 2015 this covered 5.5 million households and 17 million people (University of Manchester, 2018$_{[83]}$). In some other Asian countries, a significant proportion of senior citizens now receive a "non-contributory old age allowance" which cover about 33% of senior citizens in Bangladesh, around 50% of elderly citizens in Nepal and around three-quarters of the elderly in Hong Kong, China and Thailand (OECD, 2017$_{[74]}$; ILO, 2018$_{[84]}$). Payment rates of these social assistance pensions may be low (OECD, 2011$_{[85]}$), but they nevertheless play an important role in reducing poverty: the proliferation of these non-contributory pensions help address some of the consequences of high levels of informality in economies (ILO, 2018[84]).

- Conditional cash transfer (CCT) programmes, which provide income support to poor households that comply with certain behavioural requirements in relation to education or health (e.g. school attendance, vaccinations, health clinic visits). Apart from reducing poverty, CCTs also seek to promote equal opportunities and long-term economic growth by investing in the education and health of children. Examples includes the Benazir Income Support programme that has a conditional cash transfer component to enhance participation in education (Box 2.7).
- The Mahatma Gandhi National Rural Employment Guarantee Act (GNRES) provides Indian citizens with the right to participate in unskilled manual labour, such as building roads, canals, ponds and wells, for 100 days every fiscal year are guaranteed to all rural households (Dutta et al., 2014). The scheme promotes labour market inclusivity, gender equal pay for work of equal value and the provision of childcare facilities (Sonalde, Vashishtha and Joshi, 2015[86]; Breitkreuz et al., 2017[87]). Nevertheless, overall the role of labour market programmes is limited in the Asia Pacific region *(refs to forthcoming ADB SPI reports on Asia and Pacific)*.

In addition to these programmes, OECD policy reform evidence suggests that effective anti-poverty programmes combine income support to the poor with a range of interventions that seek to address the structural causes of poverty. Such strategies involve a multi-faceted approach to tackling the barriers to moving out of poverty, and one of the best known examples of such a policy is *Chile Solidario* which combines identification of the clients and associated income support with personal counselling and access to social services, e.g. education, employment, healthcare, housing and justice (OECD, 2009[88]).

Box 2.7. **The Benazir Income Support Programme (BISP) in Pakistan**

The Planning Commission of Pakistan adopted the country's first National Social Protection Strategy (NSPS) in 2007. In 2008, the BISP was launched as the flagship national social safety net, financed for one/third by the Pakistani government with the remainder covered by international donors.

To identify eligible households, a "poverty scorecard (PSC) method of targeting" was developed by the World Bank using the Pakistan Social and Living Standards Measurement (PSLM-4) survey data of 2005-06 (Nayab and Farooq, 2014[89]). The PSC is based on key indicators such as household size, education, child status, agricultural landholding, housing and toilet facilities, and livestock ownership. The PSC data was acquired by conducting a house-to-house survey in 2010-11. On completion of the survey, a proxy means test (PMT) formula was applied to the PSC to generate a welfare status score for every household on a scale of 0 to 100. Any household which was at a scale of 16.17 or less was considered eligible for a BISP cash transfer. Initially payments were made by post, but currently 90% of the beneficiaries receive the cash transfers through the BISP debit card.

Total cash transfers of the programme increased from 0.22% to 0.36% of GDP from 2009 to 2015, which contributed to the increase in coverage of the programme from 9.1% to 22.6% of the population of Pakistan from 2009 to 2015 (Mumtaz and Whiteford, 2017[90]).

Based on the national poverty line set by the Pakistan Bureau of Statistics, different categories of the poor population can be identified on basis of the distance of their incomes to the poverty line: ultra-poor, poor, vulnerable, quasi non-poor, and non-poor. A decrease

Box 2.7. **The Benazir Income Support Programme (BISP) in Pakistan** *(cont.)*

from 66% to 35% is observed among BISP beneficiary households in the ultra-poor and poor categories from 2011 to 2014. Out of this 31% decline in poverty, 7% of the beneficiary households moved to the vulnerable category, and 24% moved to the quasi non-poor and non-poor categories (Mumtaz and Whiteford, 2017[90]).

The primary objective of the BISP programme is to reduce the adverse impacts of the financial, food and fuel crises on the poor while the secondary objective was to increase household investments in education and health and safeguarding the vulnerable population against transient and chronic poverty. Cheema et al. (2016[91]) found evidence that the BISP is leading to an increase in per adult equivalent monthly food consumption and contributed to a reduction of wasting among girls (*see Indicator 6.3, Child Malnutrition*). The unconditional cash transfer did not affect participation in education, but it was complemented in 2012 by a conditional cash transfer which linked participation in schooling of children aged 4-12 to benefit payments "Waseela-e-Taleem (WeT)", which did increase enrolment rates (Cheema et al., 2016[92]). There are other financial supports to help clients become financially independent, including small business development and start-up supports, but their overall impact is not yet clear.

Concluding remarks

The challenges facing the development of social protection in Asia and the Pacific are manifold. In many cases current social protection spending is very low. Public social spending in Asia and the Pacific is about one-third of the OECD average and in a significant number of countries is less than one quarter or one-fifth of the OECD average. This reflects gaps in the types of programmes provided as well as gaps in coverage of existing programmes. For example, systems of support for families are lacking in many countries. Moreover, at present, most social spending is through social insurance schemes that cover (former) workers in formal employment who are comparatively well-off.

The share of informal employment in total employment varies across countries, but almost 70% of workers in the Asia/Pacific region are in informal employment, often self-employed without employees (own-account workers) and/or contributory family workers (especially in low-income countries), often working long hours for little money and in jobs that are not covered by social protection and health insurance. Youth (age 15-24) and elderly workers (over age 65) are most likely to be in informal employment. Only 30% of those with tertiary education work informally, and across Asia and the Pacific, the informal economy absorbs a large share of low-skilled workers, partly explaining its low overall level of productivity.

The already considerable challenge of extending social protection coverage to informal workers is exacerbated by changes in the nature of work and labour markets. In some economies in developing Asia about half of the jobs could be affected by automation. Many of the low-productivity jobs in Asia and the Pacific are technically "automatable" but automation may not be economically attractive given relatively low wages and high costs of investment in ICT. However, as automation will increase the demand for higher skills there is a real possibility of further labour market polarisation and increased economic inequality in the future. The response to this challenge is to increase investment in education and training in order to develop the appropriate skills for jobs complementing the new technology.

Developments in technology and automation also provide new opportunities for the extension of social protection as they can help overcome some of the administrative barriers to the receipt of benefit, payment of taxes and social security contributions. Advances in technology have at least the potential to contribute to a reduction in informality and the improvement of benefit delivery. This is important for the countries in Asia such as Bangladesh, China, India, Indonesia and Pakistan with very large populations as well as countries in the Pacific with very small populations, as in both cases natural environments pose challenges to the development, implementation and administration of social programmes.

Population ageing is an another important policy challenge, particularly in North East Asia, where rapid increases in life expectancy and even more rapid declines in fertility have resulted in the fastest rates of population ageing in history. At the same time, traditional family ties are weakening, leaving gaps in social protection that need to be addressed quickly. A further factor is that rapid income and wage growth can lead to wide gaps emerging between the retired and those working in the newer and more prosperous economy.

At present, social protection systems in the Asia Pacific are underdeveloped and mainly focused on formal workers. More should be done to protect poor families from poverty. This includes scaling up investment in social-support systems, better targeting of supports, and where possible link with existing education, health and employment support mechanisms. Countries should build on the social protection infrastructure, but given the low level of spending and taxation overall, widening the tax base and greater progressivity in taxation and financing of social insurance schemes would be important contributory factors to a greater effectiveness of national tax/benefit systems in combating poverty.

Notes

1. Employment in the manufacturing sector fell in many high-income economies over the past decades, but except for some countries in east Asia, employment in the manufacturing sector did not grow or even declined in the rest of the world – "premature deindustrialization" (Rodrik, 2015[6]).
2. Informal employees are also more likely than formal employees to engage in non-standard forms of employment: In Asia on average, 21% of employees in full-time employment hold informal jobs, but this is 60% among part-time employees, and higher still for temporary workers (ILO, 2018[25]).
3. Arntz et al. (2016[34]) also highlighted the need to take account of offsetting macro-economic adjustments, including the development of jobs that complement these new technologies, as well as the development of new jobs in the industries that actually produce the new labour-saving technologies and the associated increase in demand for these new products. Hence, the overall employment impact of future technological change may well be less than the smaller estimates.
4. It is also not entirely clear how responsive payments should be to changes in earnings or other circumstances. A more responsive system could offset short-term fluctuations in earnings, but there is evidence that low-income households may prefer to have at least one of their income sources that is predictable (Millar, 2017), and around which they can plan how to deal with other fluctuating components of their incomes.
5. All healthcare coverage under Askes (for civil servants), Jamsostek (for the private sector) and Asabri (for the police and army) were transferred to BPJS Health Care on 1 January 2014.
6. BPJS Ketenagakerjaan supersedes previous social security institutions that respectively provided old-age benefits (saving schemes and pensions) for 1) the armed forces, police personnel and civil servants employed in Military and Police Offices, 2) civil servants, 3) private employees and voluntary schemes for employees in the informal economy, and 4) healthcare and maternity benefits for civil servants, government pensioners, military and police pensioners and veterans.
7. This is built up as follows: occupational accidents – an employer-paid contribution between 0.24% and 1.74% depending on the type of business; death benefit – 0.3% paid by employers; old-age

benefit scheme 5.7% (3.7% paid by the employer; and 2% by the employee); healthcare protection scheme 5% (4% paid by employer, 1% paid by employee); and, a pension scheme 8% (4% paid by the employee and 4% by the employer).

8. There are concerns that targeted cash transfer programmes may discourage work. Banerjee et al. (2017[59]) re-analysed the data from seven randomized controlled trials of government-run cash transfer programmes in six developing countries throughout the world, and found no systematic evidence that cash transfer programmes discourage work.

References

ADB (2018), *Asian Development Outlook (ADO) 2018: How technology Affects Jobs.*, Asian Development Bank, Manila, *www.adb.org/publications/asian-development-outlook-2018-how-technology-affects-jobs* (accessed on 02 August 2018). [2]

ADB (2016), *Social Protection for Informal Workers in Asia*, Asian Development Bank, Manila, *www.adb.org/sites/default/files/publication/203891/sp-informalworkers-asia.pdf* (accessed on 10 August 2018). [12]

ADB (forthcoming), *The Social Protection Indicator – Results for Asia and the Pacific in 2015, ADB, https://spi.adb.org/spidmz/.* [15]

Adema, W., P. Fron and M. Ladaique (2014), "How much do OECD countries spend on social protection and how redistributive are their tax/benefit systems?", *International Social Security Review*, Vol. 67/1, pp. 1-25, *http://dx.doi.org/10.1111/issr.12028.* [14]

Adema, W., P. Fron and M. Ladaique (2011), "Is the European Welfare State Really More Expensive?: Indicators on Social Spending, 1980-2012; and a Manual to the OECD Social Expenditure Database (SOCX)", *OECD Social, Employment and Migration Working Papers*, No. 124, OECD Publishing, Paris, *http://dx.doi.org/10.1787/5kg2d2d4pbf0-en.* [5]

Arntz, M., T. Gregory and U. Zierahn (2016), "The Risk of Automation for Jobs in OECD Countries: A Comparative Analysis", *OECD Social, Employment and Migration Working Papers*, No. 189, OECD Publishing, Paris, *https://dx.doi.org/10.1787/5jlz9h56dvq7-en.* [45]

Australian Government (2018), *Fair Work Commission | Australia's national workplace relations tribunal, www.fwc.gov.au/* (accessed on 24 September 2018). [41]

Australian Government (2018), *Fair Work Ombudsman, www.fairwork.gov.au/* (accessed on 24 September 2018). [43]

Banerjee, A. et al. (2017), "Debunking the Stereotype of the Lazy Welfare Recipient: Evidence from Cash Transfer Programs", *The World Bank Research Observer*, Vol. 32/2, pp. 155-184, *http://dx.doi.org/10.1093/wbro/lkx002.* [80]

Banerjee, S. (2016), *Digital Dividends Aadhaar: Digital Inclusion and Public Services in India, http://pubdocs.worldbank.org/en/655801461250682317/WDR16-BP-Aadhaar-Paper-Banerjee.pdf* (accessed on 20 August 2018). [54]

Barrientos, A. (2016), *Social assistance in developing countries.*, Cambridge Univ Press, *http://admin.cambridge.org/sb/academic/subjects/politics-international-relations/political-economy/social-assistance-developing-countries* (accessed on 23 August 2018). [79]

Bassanini, A. and E. Caroli (2014), "Is Work Bad for Health? The Role of Constraint vs Choice", *IZA Disussion Papers*, No. 7891, Forschungsinstitut zur Zukunft der Arbeit, *https://basepub.dauphine.fr/bitstream/handle/123456789/12483/dp7891.pdf?sequence=3&isAllowed=y* (accessed on 04 September 2018). [35]

BBC (2018), *Aadhaar: India top court upholds world's largest biometric scheme – BBC News, www.bbc.com/news/world-asia-india-44777787* (accessed on 27 September 2018). [51]

Berg, J. (2016), "Income security in the on-demand economy: Findings and policy lessons from a survey of crowdworkers", *Conditions of Work and Employment Series* , No. 74, ILO, *www.ilo.org/publns* (accessed on 23 October 2018). [66]

Bonnet, F. (2019), *Facts on Business Informality*, ILO. [33]

Breitkreuz, R. et al. (2017), "The Mahatma Gandhi National Rural Employment Guarantee Scheme: A Policy Solution to Rural Poverty in India?", *Development Policy Review, http://dx.doi.org/10.1111/dpr.12220.* [87]

Burgstaller, S. et al. (2017), "*Rethinking Mobility: The 'pay as you go' car: Ride hailing just the start*", Goldman Sachs, *www.gs.com/research/hedge.html* (accessed on 28 September 2018). [57]

Card, D. and J. Dinardo (2002), "Skill-Biased Technological Change and Rising Wage Inequality: Some Problems and Puzzles", *Journal of Labor Economics*, Vol. 20/4, *http://davidcard.berkeley.edu/papers/skill-tech-change.pdf* (accessed on 25 September 2018). [47]

Cheema, I. et al. (2016), *Evaluation of the Waseela-e-Taleem Conditional Cash Transfer Programme 2016 Benazir Income Support Programme*, Oxford Policy Management, *http://bisp.gov.pk/wp-content/uploads/2017/02/WET-Report.pdf* (accessed on 22 November 2018). [92]

Cheema, I. et al. (2016), *Benazir Income Support Programme Final Impact Evaluation Report*, Oxford Policy Management, *www.opml.co.uk* (accessed on 22 November 2018). [91]

Chen, M. (2012), "The Informal Economy: Definitions, Theories and Policies WIEGO Working Papers", *WIEGO Working Paper*, No. 1, Women in Informal Employment: Globalizing and Organizing (WIEGO), *www.wiego.org/sites/default/files/publications/files/Chen_WIEGO_WP1.pdf* (accessed on 07 August 2018). [26]

Department Statistics of Malaysia (2015), *Road Injury statistics*, *www.miros.gov.my/1/page.php?id=17*. [62]

Eurostat (2016), *European system of integrated social protection statistics – ESSPROS*, Publications Office of the European Union, Luxembourg, *http://ec.europa.eu/eurostat/documents/3859598/7766647/KS-GQ-16-010-EN-N.pdf/3fe2216e-13b0-4ba1-b84f-a7d5b091235f* (accessed on 09 December 2017). [7]

Ford, M. and V. Honan (2017), "The Go-Jek Effect", in Jurriens, E. and Tapsell, R. (ed.), *Digital Indonesia: Connectivity and Divergence*. [59]

Frey, C. and M. Osborne (2013), "The Future of Employment", Oxford Martin School, University of Oxford, *www.oxfordmartin.ox.ac.uk/downloads/academic/future-of-employment.pdf* (accessed on 24 September 2018). [44]

Guardian, T. (2018), *"Modicare": India's PM promises free health care for poorest citizens, World news, The Guardian*, *www.theguardian.com/world/2018/sep/24/modicare-indias-pm-promises-free-health-care-for-half-a-billion-people* (accessed on 01 October 2018). [77]

Holmes, A. (2017), *How big is the transport sharing economy?*, *https://daliaresearch.com/how-big-is-the-transport-sharing-economy/* (accessed on 28 September 2018). [55]

Hussmanns, R. (2004), "Measuring the informal economy: From employment in the informal sector to informal employment", *ILO Working Paper*, No. 53, International Labour Office, Geneva, *www.ilo.org/wcmsp5/groups/public/---dgreports/---integration/documents/publication/wcms_079142.pdf* (accessed on 07 August 2018). [27]

ILO (2018), *Informality and non-standard forms of employment*, ILO, *www.ilo.org/wcmsp5/groups/public/---dgreports/---inst/documents/publication/wcms_646040.pdf* (accessed on 27 November 2018). [67]

ILO (2018), *Social protection for older persons: Policy trends and statistics 2017-19*, ILO, Geneva, *www.ilo.org/publns* (accessed on 28 September 2018). [84]

ILO (2018), *Women and men in the informal economy: a statistical picture – third edition*, International Labour office, Geneva, *www.ilo.org/wcmsp5/groups/public/---dgreports/---dcomm/documents/publication/wcms_626831.pdf* (accessed on 07 August 2018). [28]

ILO (2017), *World Social Protection Report 2017-19: Universal social protection to achieve the Sustainable Development Goals*, International Labour Organization, Geneva, *www.social-protection.org/gimi/gess/RessourcePDF.action?ressource.ressourceId=54887* (accessed on 03 September 2018). [9]

ILO (2016), *Child Money Programme Mongolia*, ILO, Geneva, *www.ilo.org/wcmsp5/groups/public/---asia/---ro-bangkok/---ilo-beijing/documents/publication/wcms_534930.pdf* (accessed on 28 September 2018). [81]

ILO (2016), *World Employment and Social Outlook 2016: Transforming jobs to end poverty*, ILO, Geneva, *www.ilo.org/global/research/global-reports/weso/2016-transforming-jobs/WCMS_481534/lang--en/index.htm* (accessed on 27 November 2018). [30]

ILO (2005), *ILO Social Security Inquiry*, *www.socialsecurityextension.org/gimi/gess/RessourcePDF.do?ressource. ressourceId=6622* (accessed on 09 December 2017). [8]

ILR School and Future of Work Initiative (2018), *Gig Economy Data Hub*, Cornell University. Industrial and Labor Relations School, The Aspen Institute, Future of Work Initiative, *www.gigeconomydata.org/* (accessed on 27 September 2018). [64]

Jonasson, E. (2012), "Government Effectiveness and Regional Variation in Informal Employment", *Journal of Development Studies*, Vol. 48/4, pp. 481-497, *http://dx.doi.org/10.1080/00220388.2011.615922*. [31]

Jütting, J. and J. De Laiglesia (2009), *Is Informal Normal? Towards More and Better Jobs in Developing Countries*, *www.oecd.org/publishing/corrigenda* (accessed on 22 November 2018). [29]

Katz, L. and A. Krueger (2016), "The Rise and Nature of Alternative Work Arrangements in the United States, 1995-2015", *NBER Working Paper*, No. 22667, National Bureau of Economic Research, Cambridge, MA, *http://dx.doi.org/10.3386/w22667*. [65]

Limer, E. (2014), *My Brief and Curious Life As a Mechanical Turk*, *https://gizmodo.com/my-brief-and-curious-life-as-a-mechanical-turk-1587864671* (accessed on 27 September 2018). [50]

Marciano, J. (2016), *Who Runs the World? Uber!*, *www.similarweb.com/blog/worldwide-ride-hailing-apps*. [56]

Mumtaz, Z. and P. Whiteford (2017), "Social safety nets in the development of a welfare system in Pakistan: An analysis of the Benazir Income Support Programme", *Asia Pacific Journal of Public Administration*, Vol. 39/1, pp. 16-38, *http://dx.doi.org/10.1080/23276665.2017.1290902*. [90]

Muralidharan, K., P. Niehaus and S. Sukhtankar (2017), *Direct Benefits Transfer in Food Results from One Year of Process Monitoring in Union Territories*, UC San Diego, *http://econweb.ucsd.edu/~kamurali/papers/Other%20Writing/20170905_UT_DBT_Report.pdf* (accessed on 20 August 2018). [53]

Muralidharan, K., P. Niehaus and S. Sukhtankar (2016), "Building State Capacity: Evidence from Biometric Smartcards in India†", *American Economic Review*, Vol. 106/10, pp. 2895-2929, *http://dx.doi.org/10.1257/aer.20141346*. [52]

Nayab, D. and S. Farooq (2014), "Effectiveness of Cash Transfer Programmes for Household Welfare in Pakistan: The Case of the Benazir Income Support Programme", *The Pakistan Development Review*, Vol. 53/2, pp. 145-174, *www.pide.org.pk/pdf/PDR/2014/Volume2/145-174.pdf* (accessed on 01 October 2018). [89]

Nedelkoska, L. and G. Quintini (2018), "Automation, skills use and training", *OECD Social, Employment and Migration Working Papers*, No. 202, OECD Publishing, Paris, *http://dx.doi.org/10.1787/2e2f4eea-en*. [46]

OECD (2019), *The Social Expenditure Database (SOCX) Manual – 2019 Edition*, *www.oecd.org/social/expenditure.htm*. [6]

OECD (2018), *Economic Outlook for Southeast Asia, China and India 2018 Fostering Growth Through Digitalisation*, OECD Publishing, Paris, *http://dx.doi.org/10/9789264286184-en*. [3]

OECD (2018), *Good Jobs for all in a Changing World of Work: The OECD Jobs Strategy – Meeting of the OECD Council at Ministerial Level*, OECD, Paris, *www.oecd.org/mcm/documents/C-MIN-2018-7-EN.pdf* (accessed on 06 August 2018). [24]

OECD (2018), *Good Jobs for All in a Changing World of Work: The OECD Jobs Strategy*, OECD Publishing, Paris, *https://dx.doi.org/10.1787/9789264308817-en*. [25]

OECD (2018), *OECD Economic Outlook, Volume 2018, Issue 1*, OECD Publishing, Paris, *https://dx.doi.org/10.1787/eco_outlook-v2018-1-en*. [1]

OECD (2018), *OECD Economic Surveys: Indonesia 2018*, OECD Publishing, Paris, *https://dx.doi.org/10.1787/eco_surveys-idn-2018-en*. [76]

OECD (2018), *Opportunities for All: A Framework for Policy Action on Inclusive Growth*, OECD Publishing, Paris, *http://dx.doi.org/10.1787/9789264301665-en*. [21]

OECD (2018), *Putting faces to the jobs at risk of automation*, *www.oecd.org/employment/future-of-work.htm* (accessed on 06 August 2018). [18]

OECD (2018), *Revenue Statistics 2018*, OECD Publishing, Paris, *https://dx.doi.org/10.1787/rev_stats-2018-en*. [10]

OECD (2018), *Revenue Statistics in Asian and Pacific Economies*, OECD Publishing, Paris, *https://dx.doi.org/10.1787/9789264308091-en*. [11]

OECD (2018), *The Future of Social Protection: What works for non-standard workers?*, OECD Policy Brief on the Future of Work, Paris, *www.oecd.org/employment/future-of-work.htm* (accessed on 24 September 2018). [19]

OECD (2018), *The Future of Social Protection: What Works for Non-standard Workers?*, OECD Publishing, Paris, *https://dx.doi.org/10.1787/9789264306943-en*. [48]

OECD (2017), *A Decade of Social Protection Development in Selected Asian Countries*, OECD Publishing, Paris, *http://dx.doi.org/10.1787/9789264272262-en*. [74]

OECD (2017), *Basic income as a policy option: Can it add up?*, OECD, Paris, *www.oecd.org/social/Basic-Income-Policy-Option-2017.pdf* (accessed on 20 November 2018). [69]

OECD (2017), *Future of Work and Skills*, OECD, Paris, *www.oecd.org/els/emp/wcms_556984.pdf* (accessed on 06 November 2018). [17]

OECD (2017), *Revenue Statistics in Asian Countries 2017: Trends in Indonesia, Japan, Kazakhstan, Korea, Malaysia, the Philippines and Singapore*, OECD Publishing, Paris, *https://dx.doi.org/10.1787/9789264278943-en*. [13]

OECD (2016), *OECD Employment Outlook 2016*, OECD Publishing, Paris, *http://dx.doi.org/10.1787/empl_outlook-2016-en*. [36]

OECD (2015), *Focus on – Minimum wages after the crisis: Making them pay*, *www.oecd.org/social/Focus-on-Minimum-Wages-after-the-crisis-2015.pdf* (accessed on 25 September 2018). [39]

OECD (2015), *In It Together: Why Less Inequality Benefits All*, OECD Publishing, Paris, *http://dx.doi.org/10.1787/9789264235120-en*. [38]

OECD (2015), *OECD Employment Outlook 2015*, OECD Publishing, Paris, *http://dx.doi.org/10.1787/empl_outlook-2015-en*. [23]

OECD (2014), *OECD Employment Outlook 2014*, OECD Publishing, Paris, *http://dx.doi.org/10.1787/empl_outlook-2014-en*. [22]

OECD (2012), *Reducing opportunities for tax non-compliance in the underground economy*, OECD, Paris, *www.oecd.org/tax/forum-on-tax-administration/publications-and-products/sme/49427993.pdf* (accessed on 22 November 2018). [34]

OECD (2011), *OECD Employment Outlook 2011*, OECD Publishing, Paris, *https://doi.org/10.1787/19991266*. [85]

OECD (2009), *OECD Reviews of Labour Market and Social Policies: Chile 2009*, OECD Reviews of Labour Market and Social Policies, OECD Publishing, Paris, *http://dx.doi.org/10.1787/9789264060616-en*. [88]

OECD (2000), *Pushing Ahead with Reform in Korea*, OECD Publishing, Paris, *www.oecd.org* (accessed on 28 September 2018). [73]

Pathways for Prosperity Commission (2018), *Charting Pathways for Inclusive Growth – From Paralysis to Preparation*, *www.click.co.uk* (accessed on 15 October 2018). [20]

Pesole, A. et al. (2018), *Platform Workers in Europe Evidence from the COLLEEM Survey*, European Union, Joint Research Centre, *http://dx.doi.org/10.2760/742789*. [49]

Prabowo, Y. (2018), *Uber, Go-Jek, Grab: What do People in Indonesia Actually Want from Ride-Hailing Apps?*, ecommerceIQ, *https://ecommerceiq.asia/cp-ride-hailing-apps-in-indonesia/* (accessed on 27 September 2018). [61]

Prinja, S. et al. (2017), "Impact of Publicly Financed Health Insurance Schemes on Healthcare Utilization and Financial Risk Protection in India: A Systematic Review", *PLOS ONE*, Vol. 12/2, pp. e0170996, *http://dx.doi.org/10.1371/journal.pone.0170996*. [78]

Puri, R. (2017), "India's National Food Security Act (NFSA): Early Experiences", *Lansa Working Paper Series*, No. 14, *www.lansasouthasia.org* (accessed on 01 October 2018). [82]

Purnell, N. (2016), *Uber Rival Grab Gains Ground in Southeast Asia*, wall Street Journal, *www.wsj.com/articles/uber-rival-grab-seizes-lead-in-southeast-asia-146762050*. [58]

Queisser, M., A. Reilly and Y. Hu (2016), "China's pension system and reform: An OECD perspective", *Economic and Political Studies*, Vol. 4/4, pp. 345-367, *http://dx.doi.org/10.1080/20954816.2016.1251134*. [71]

Rodrik, D. (2015), "Premature Deindustrialization", *NBER Working Paper Series*, No. 20935, National Bureau of Economic Research, *www.nber.org/papers/w20935* (accessed on 22 October 2018). [16]

Salditt, F., P. Whiteford and W. Adema (2008), "Pension reform in China", *International Social Security Review*, Vol. 61/3, pp. 47-71, *http://dx.doi.org/10.1111/j.1468-246X.2008.00316.x*. [70]

Social Security Organisation of Malaysia (2018), *Self-Employed Employment Injury Scheme*, *www.perkeso.gov.my/index.php/en/our-services/benefits/self-employed-employment-injury-scheme-taxi* (accessed on 27 September 2018). [63]

Sonalde, D., P. Vashishtha and O. Joshi (2015), *Majatma Gandhi National Rural Employment Guarantee Act: A Catalysus for Rural Transformation*, *www.esocialsciences.org/Articles/show_Article.aspx?qs=ebKFqzOKbXo7se0+tFTcFgB/Qg9lMx8H7EcQyowRRVbAjv2BNHkaakHzcZy9fkFLyG2jMM/EOSe03zMtemCj/anx+TrNLBXx/i6DN60i0h8=*. [86]

Statistics Korea (2017), *Statistics Korea Portal*, *www.index.go.kr/main.do?cate=7* (accessed on 16 December 2017). [75]

Stewart, A. et al. (2016), *Creighton and Stewart's labour law*, The Federation Press, *www.federationpress.com.au/bookstore/book.asp?isbn=9781760020552*. [42]

University of Manchester (2018), *Social Assistance Explorer*, *www.social-assistance.manchester.ac.uk/* (accessed on 28 September 2018). [83]

Weng, X. (2015), "The rural informal economy – Understanding drivers and livelihood impacts in agriculture, timber and mining", *IIED Working Paper*, International Institute for Environment [32] and Development, *www.iied.org@iiedwww.facebook.com/theIIEDhttp://pubs.iied.org/16590IIED* (accessed on 23 October 2018).

Whiteford, P. (2017), *Social security and welfare spending in Australia: Assessing long-term trends*, Australian National University, Crawford School of Public Policy TTPI Tax and Transfer Policy Institute, *www.anu.edu.au* (accessed on 25 September 2018). [37]

WHO Global Health Observatory (2018), *Road traffic injuries*, WHO, *www.who.int/violence_injury_prevention/road_traffic/en/* (accessed on 27 September 2018). [60]

World Bank Group (2018), *The State of Social Safety Nets*, World Bank Group, *https://openknowledge.worldbank.org/bitstream/handle/10986/29115/9781464812545.pdf?sequence=5&isAllowed=y* (accessed on 15 October 2018). [68]

World Bank Group (2018), *World Development Report 2019: The Changing Nature of Work.*, Washington, DC, World Bank Group, *https://openknowledge.worldbank.org/handle/10986/30435* (accessed on 06 November 2018). [4]

Wright, C. and R. Lansbury (2016), "Employment relations in Australia --", in Bamber G.J., Lansbury R.D., W. (ed.), *International and comparative employment relations: National regulation, global changes*, Allen & Unwin/Sage, London. [40]

Zhu, H. and A. Walker (2018), "Pension system reform in China: Who gets what pensions?", *Social Policy & Administration*, *http://dx.doi.org/10.1111/spol.12368*. [72]

Society at a Glance
Asia/Pacific 2019
© OECD 2019

Chapter 3

General context indicators

GDP PER CAPITA

Gross domestic product per person (**GDP per capita**) varies considerably across the Asia/Pacific region (Figure 3.1). Differences in GDP per capita within the Asia/Pacific region are large: Macau, China's GDP per capita is more than 100 times higher than in Nepal and Tajikistan. GDP per capita is well above the OECD average (USD 38 200) in the richest economies in the region: Australia, Hong Kong, China, Macau, China, New Zealand and Singapore. By contrast, more than two-thirds of the Asia/Pacific economies have a GDP per capita that is below the regional average (USD 13 800).

Real annual average growth rates of GDP per capita for the Asia/Pacific region have fallen a little between 2007 and 2017 (Figure 3.2). Over this period, real annual average growth rates ranged from negative growth in Brunei Darussalam and Timor-Leste to strong growth (at over 5.0% annually) in Bangladesh, China, India, Lao PDR, Mongolia and Myanmar.

Across the Asia/Pacific region, the annual average growth rate over the 2012-17 period (0.9%) was far smaller than over the previous 5 years (1.7% between 2007 and 2012). This slowdown is largely related to substantially reduced growth rates among countries that grew rapidly during the 2007-12 period (i.e. Azerbaijan, Brunei Darussalam, Macau (China), Mongolia, Sri Lanka and Timor-Leste). By comparison, GDP per capita increased in recent years across the OECD on average.

Poorer countries in the Asia/pacific region **tend to grow at a faster** rate than richer ones (Figure 3.3), although the pace over the period of 2012-17 has slowed compared to the previous years (2006-12). There is a negative correlation between the pace of growth in GDP per capita over the period 2012-17 and the initial level in 2012. This suggest there is some evidence for economic theories of "catch-up" and GDP convergence. China and Indonesia are growing more rapidly than one might expect given it is level of GDP, while the opposite holds for Tajikistan.

Definition and measurement

Among the different measures available in the System of National Accounts (SNA), gross domestic product (GDP) per capita is the one most commonly used for comparing the sizes of economies across countries. GDP per capita measures the sum of marketed goods and services produced within the national boundary, averaged across everyone who lives within this territory.

GDP per capita is calculated using a country's GDP in 2017 United States dollars (USD) which is then divided by the country's total population. Real annual average growth is calculated using a country's GDP per capita in constant 2010 USD as compound annual growth rate during the period (2007-17, 2007-12, and 2012-17). Level log of GDP per capita is calculated by using common log for the GDP per capital of the reference year (2012).

The data come from the World Bank, World Development Indicators (*http://data.worldbank.org/indicator*) and OECD statistics (*http://dotstat.oecd.org*).

Figure 3.1. **GDP per capita varies considerably across the Asia/Pacific region**

Current GDP per capita (↘), 2017 (2017 USD)

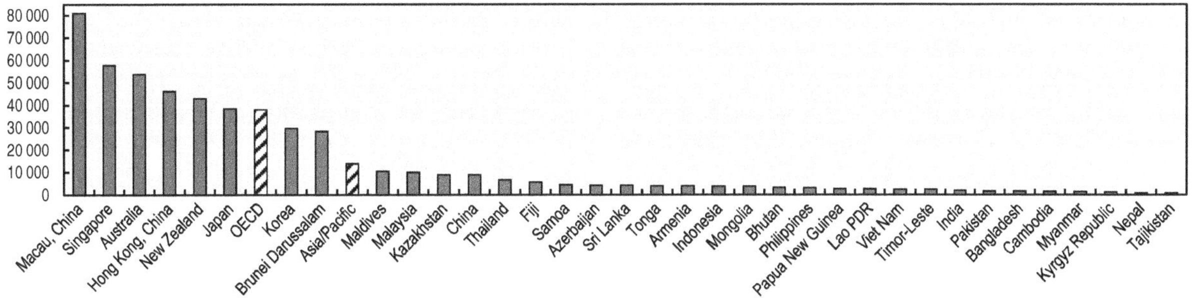

Source: *World Bank, World Development Indicators, http://data.worldbank.org/indicator.*

StatLink http://dx.doi.org/10.1787/888933899736

Figure 3.2. **Many Asian economies continue to grow at pace, but the rate of growth has declined somewhat in recent years**

Real annual average growth rate of GDP per capita, 2007-17

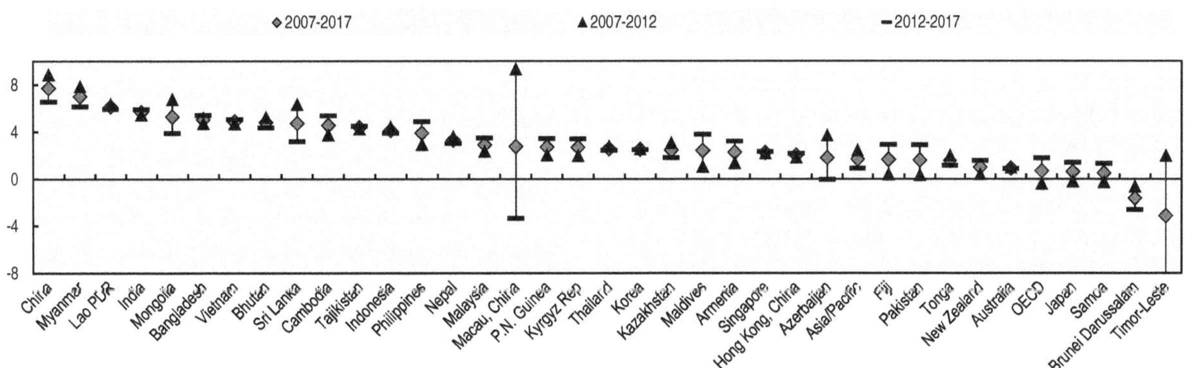

Source: *World Bank, World Development Indicators, http://data.worldbank.org/indicator.*

StatLink http://dx.doi.org/10.1787/888933899755

Figure 3.3. **Poorer countries in the Asia/Pacific tend to grow faster than richer ones**

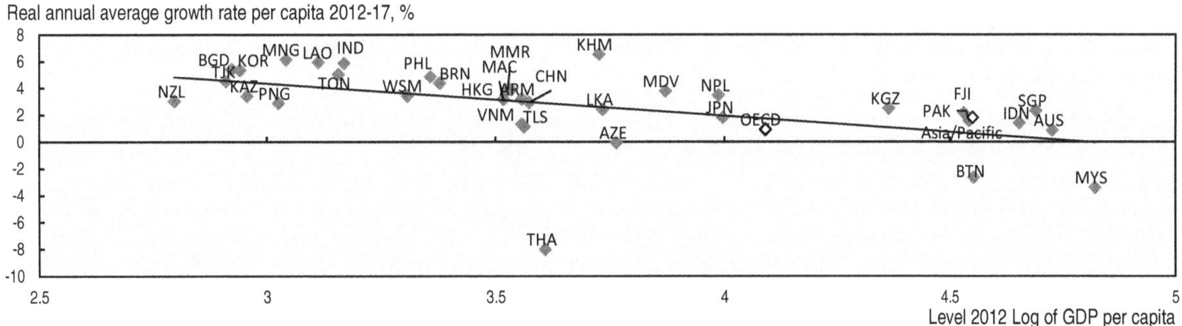

Source: *World Bank, World Development Indicators, http://data.worldbank.org/indicator.*

StatLink http://dx.doi.org/10.1787/888933899774

FERTILITY

The **total fertility rate (TFR)** gives an indication of the number of children an average woman will have in her lifetime. The size of the population remains stable if the total fertility rate is a little over two, allowing for some mortality during infancy and childhood. This so-called "replacement rate" is around 2.1 children per women for industrialised countries but it may be higher for poorer countries.

Total fertility rates **vary considerably in the Asia/Pacific region** (Figure 3.4). In 2016, women in the region had on average 2.4 children compared with OECD countries at 1.7 children. Fertility rates in island countries such as Timor-Leste and Samoa are high with women having four children or more on average. By contrast, fertility rates are lowest in Korea and Singapore at around 1 child per woman. Armenia, China, Japan, Thailand, Hong Kong (China) and Macau (China) all also have TFRs that are below the OECD average.

Birth rates have declined sharply over the last decades. The TFR average across the Asia/Pacific region fell by almost 3 children per woman from 1970 to 2016. OECD member countries in the region, with the exception of Korea, experienced a slower decline in the TFR at less than 1.5 children per woman on average. The Maldives recorded the largest decline in the TFR, from over seven children per woman in 1970 to 2.1 in 2016. No country had higher TFRs in 2016 than in 1970. Kazakhstan and Macau, China, are the two only economies which had higher TFRs in 2016 than in 1995.

Women in **poor economies** have much higher fertility rates than women in **wealthier economies** (Figure 3.5). In 2016, women in OECD and East Asian economies had the fewest children compared with the greater Asia/Pacific region. As more women gain higher educational attainment and pursue labour market careers, they tend to postpone having children and/or have less children altogether.

In countries where birth rates for **adolescent girls** are high – and where many young people are married (see Marriage and divorce), overall fertility rates are also relatively high (Figure 3.6). Adolescent fertility rates are lowest in Korea and the Korea DPR. They remain high at around 60 births per 1 000 women aged 15-19 in Lao DPR; Nepal and the Philippines. They are highest in Bangladesh at 85 births per 1 000 women aged 15-19, almost three times the Asia/Pacific average (29 per 1 000) and over six times more than the OECD average (13 per 1 000).

Definition and measurement

The total fertility rate (TFR) in a specific year corresponds to the number of children that would be born to each woman if she were to live to the end of her childbearing years and if the likelihood of her giving birth to children at each life stage followed the currently prevailing age-specific fertility rates. The adolescent birth rate is defined as the annual number of births per 1 000 women aged 15 to 19.

The data presented here are extracted from the World Bank's World Development Indicators which for population data uses the United Nations Population Statistics as its key source (*http://esa.un.org/wpp*). These population statistics are based on administrative "vital registration" data, census data and/or survey data, and the quality of these sources is likely to vary across countries. For GDP per capita, see previous indicator "GDP per capita".

Further reading

United Nations (2017), World Fertility Data 2017 (POP/DB/*Fert/Rev2017*).

OECD (2018), "SF2 .1 Fertility rates", *OECD Family Database*, *http://oe.cd/fdb*.

Figure 3.4. **Despite rapid declines, fertility rates in Asia/Pacific are still higher than in OECD**

Number of children per woman aged 15 to 49, in 1970, 1995 and 2016 or nearest years

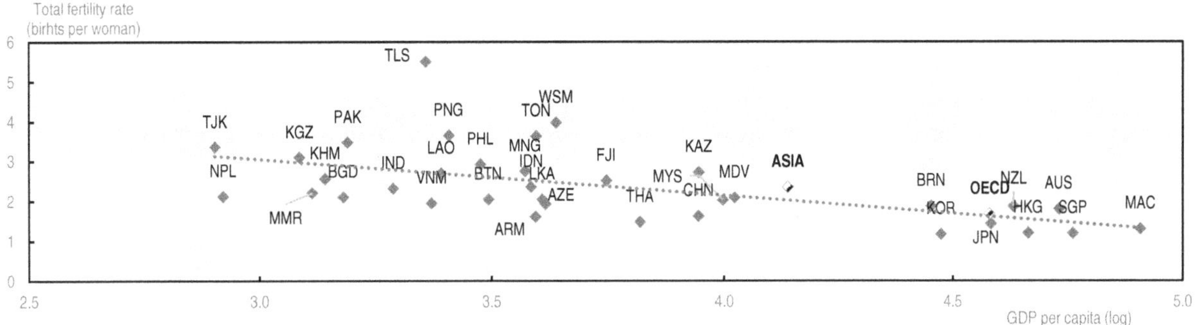

Source: *World Bank, world Development Indicators, http://data.worldbank.org/indicator.*

StatLink http://dx.doi.org/10.1787/888933899793

Figure 3.5. **Richer countries have lower fertility rates**

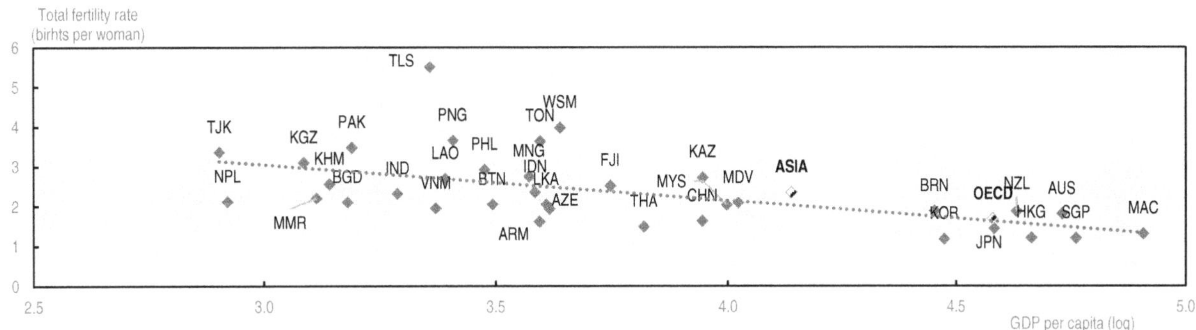

Source: *World Bank, world Development Indicators, http://data.worldbank.org/indicator.*

StatLink http://dx.doi.org/10.1787/888933899812

Figure 3.6. **Countries with high fertility tend to also have high adolescent birth rates**

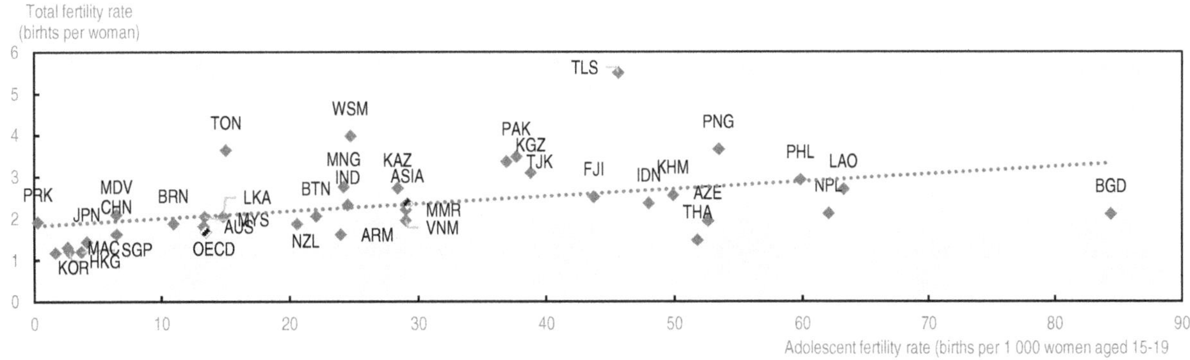

Source: *World Bank, world Development Indicators, http://data.worldbank.org/indicator.*

StatLink http://dx.doi.org/10.1787/888933899831

MARRIAGE AND DIVORCE

Both **marriage and divorce rates have increased** in the Asia/Pacific region since 2000 (Figure 3.7 and Figure 3.8). Crude marriage rates of Asia/Pacific countries are almost twice as high as the average across OECD countries whilst crude divorce rates are half of the OECD average. Crude marriage rates are highest at over nine marriages per 1 000 adults in China, Kazakhstan and Tajikistan; they are around four marriages per 1 000 adults in Australia, New Zealand and Thailand. Since 2000, crude divorce rates have increased in most Asia/Pacific countries, but not among the OECD countries in the Asia/Pacific region (Australia, Japan, Korea and New Zealand). Overall, countries with higher crude marriage rates tend to have higher crude divorce rates.

Across the Asia/Pacific the **mean age of first marriage** has increased by 3 years on average since 1990 (Figure 3.9), In 1990, the mean age at first marriage across the selected Asia/Pacific economies was 23.5 years for women and 26.1 years for men. By 2016, this average age had increased to 26.6 years for women and to 29.1 years for men, still some 3 to 4 years below the OECD average for men and women. A strong tendency of postponing marriages is observed across Asia/Pacific economies, but large cross-national differences remain: since 1990, the mean age at first marriage has increased by more than five years among men and women in Korea and Viet Nam, while change was much more limited in Azerbaijan and Tajikistan, where the mean age of first marriage for women increased by less than a year.

Definition and measurement

The crude marriage rate is defined as the number of legal civil unions or marriages each year per 1 000 people. The crude divorce rate (CDR), defined as the number of legal civil unions or marriages that are dissolved each year per 1 000 people.

The mean age at first marriage is defined as the mean average age in years of marrying persons at the time of first marriage. This measure is disaggregated by gender with separate averages for men and women.

The crude marriage rate is the number of marriages formed each year as a ratio to 1 000 adults; similarly, the crude divorce rate is the number of marriages dissolved in a given year as related to the total adult population. The data were taken from the 2006 and 2016 UN Demographic Yearbook of the UN department of Economic and Social Affairs Statistics Division.

Figure 3.7. In most countries, marriage rates increased since 2000

Crude marriage rates, per 1 000 persons, 2000 and 2016 or the latest year

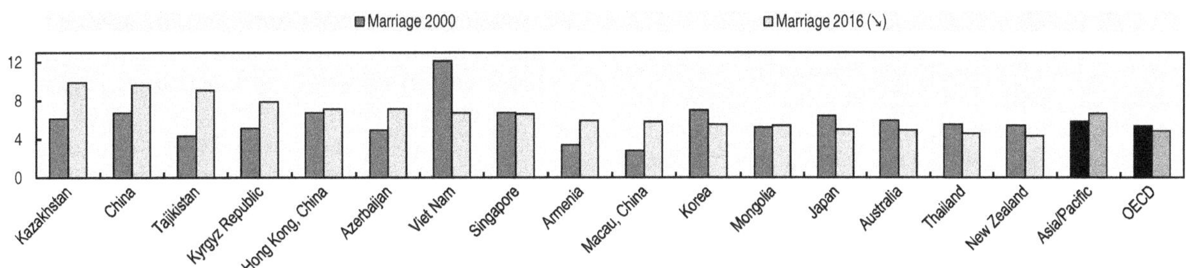

Source: *UN Demographic Yearbook, https://unstats.un.org/unsd/demographic/products/dyb/default.htm.*

StatLink http://dx.doi.org/10.1787/888933899850

Figure 3.8. In most countries, divorce rates increased since 2000

Crude divorce rates, per 1 000 persons, 2000 and 2016 or the latest year

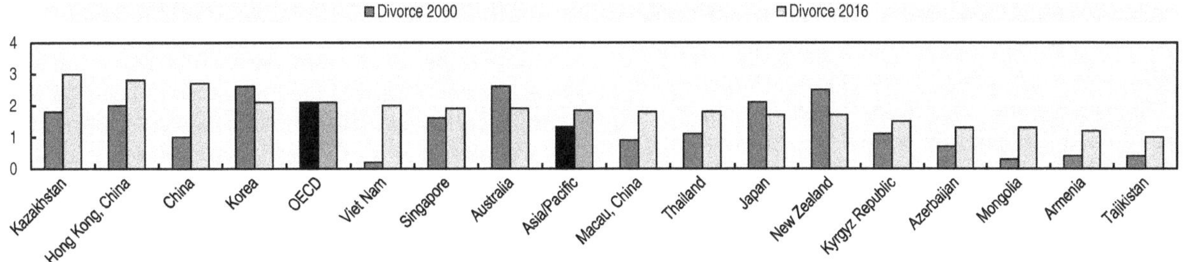

Source: *UN Demographic Yearbook, https://unstats.un.org/unsd/demographic/products/dyb/default.htm.*

StatLink http://dx.doi.org/10.1787/888933899869

Figure 3.9. The mean age of first marriage has increased by 3 years since 1990

The mean age of first marriage, 1990 and 2016 or the latest year

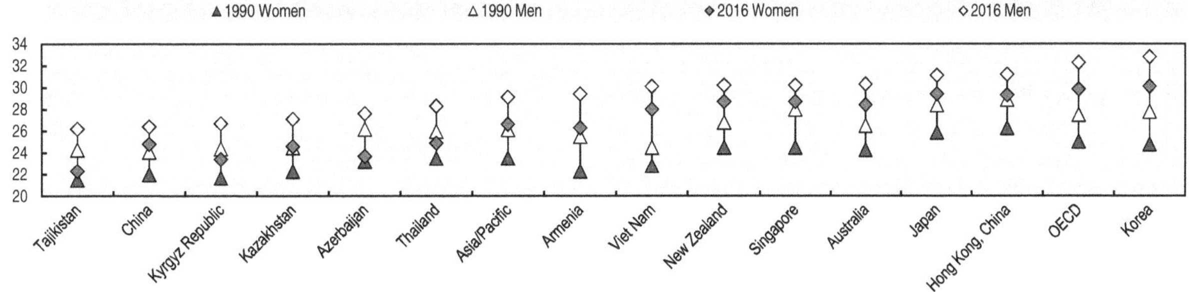

Note: All countries are in 1990 except Estonia (1992) and Poland (1993), and Chile, France, Latvia, Mexico, and Slovak Republic are not included in OECD average. All countries are in 2016 except Mexico (2014), Chile, France, Ireland, Israel, and United Kingdom (2015). Canada and Iceland are not included in OECD average.

Source: *OECD/Korea Family Database, OECD Family Database, UN Demographic Yearbook, https://unstats.un.org/unsd/demographic/products/dyb/default.htm.*

StatLink http://dx.doi.org/10.1787/888933899888

INTERNATIONAL MIGRATION

The total **refugee stock** including asylum seekers to the Asia/Pacific area has decreased from 3.9 million in 1990 to 2.6 million in 2017 – data do not account for the recent Rohingya crisis with refugee flows from Myanmar to Bangladesh and India. Over the same period the number of refugees in OECD countries has more than tripled to 7.3 million (Figure 3.10). The decline of the number of refugees in Pakistan (1.9 million) contributed to the overall decline in the refugee stock in the Asia/Pacific region. By contrast, the number of refugees increased by more than 100 000 in India and more than 10 000 in China, Indonesia, Japan, Nepal and Thailand.

The share of **migrant flows from the Asia/Pacific to OECD** countries among total inflows to the OECD (around 27%) is largely unchanged, even though the absolute number has doubled over the 2000 to 2016 period (Figure 3.11). More than half of the immigrants to the OECD came from China, India, and Viet Nam in 2016. In 2017, migrants from the Asia/Pacific region have relatively high employment rate, for example in Canada (72.8%), EU 28 (64.69%), and the United States (69.35), but the situation differs sharply across migrant groups and countries of origin within the region (OECD, 2015; forthcoming). Women are less likely to be employed than men, and employment rates of migrants increase significantly with level of educational attainment (OECD, 2015).

Migration remittance flows to Asia and the Pacific have continuously increased since 2000, except during the Great Recession (2008/9). Among all **remittances sent to Asian/Pacific countries** in 2017, approximately two/thirds are destined for India (26%), China (24%), and the Philippines (21%) (Figure 3.12). Remittances sent by Asian/Pacific migrants to their countries of origin amounted to USD 267 billion in 2017, accounting for more than one third of all global remittance flows (USD 613 billion). Remittances constitute a significant share of gross domestic product in some of the countries of origin, as for example in the Kyrgyz Republic (33%), Nepal (28%), Tajikistan (31%) and Tonga (34%).

Definition and measurement

An asylum seeker is someone who applies for international protection, but whose claim has not been definitely evaluated. National asylum systems may decide which asylum seekers actually qualify for international protection. Those judged through paper procedures not to be refugees, nor to be in need of any other form of international protection, can be sent back to their home countries. The total refugee stock, used for measure this indicator, includes asylum seeks to the Asia/Pacific region. Data on the total refugee stock (including asylum seekers) are from the United Nations, Department of Economic and Social Affairs, Population Division (2017).

Immigrant flows from the Asia/Pacific to the OECD countries measures the number of people move to the OECD from the Asia/Pacific countries each year. Data on this indicator are from OECD International Migration Database. A remittance is a transfer of money by a foreign work to an individual in his or her country of origin. Data on migrant remittance inflows in current (nominal) USD are from the World Bank Migration and Remittance Data (Figure 3.12).

Further reading

OECD (2015), Connecting with Emigrants: A Global Profile of Diasporas 2015, OECD Publishing, Paris, *http://dx.doi.org/10.1787/9789264239845-en.*

OECD/ADBI/ILO (2018), Labor Migration in Asia: Increasing the Development Impact of Migration through Finance and Technology, ADBI, Tokyo, *https://doi.org/10.1787/9789264289642-en.*

OECD (forthcoming), International Migration Outlook 2018, OECD Publishing, Paris.

Figure 3.10. **The total number of refugee stock (including asylum seekers) declined in Asia/Pacific though OECD countries recorded an unprecedented number of 7.3 million**

Estimated refugee stock (including asylum seekers) in OECD, Asia/Pacific, and Pakistan

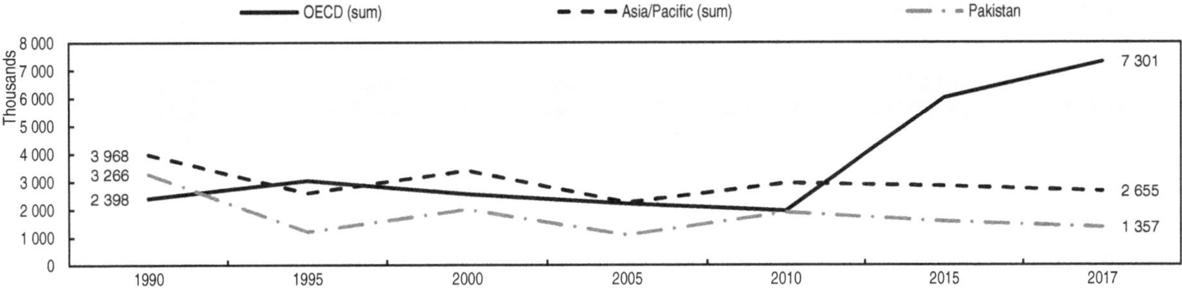

Note: The Asia/Pacific (sum) does not include Bhutan, Brunei Darussalam, Korea DPR, Lao PDR, Myanmar, and Tonga as well as Viet Nam for 2016 and 2017 due to the lack of data.

Source: United Nations, Department of Economic and Social Affairs, Population Division (2017). Trends in International Migrant Stock: The 2017 Revision (United Nations Database, POP/DB/IMIG/Stock/Rev/2017).

StatLink http://dx.doi.org/10.1787/888933899907

Figure 3.11. **Migrant flows from the Asia/Pacific to the OECD almost doubled after 2000**

Inflows of foreign population by nationality (million)

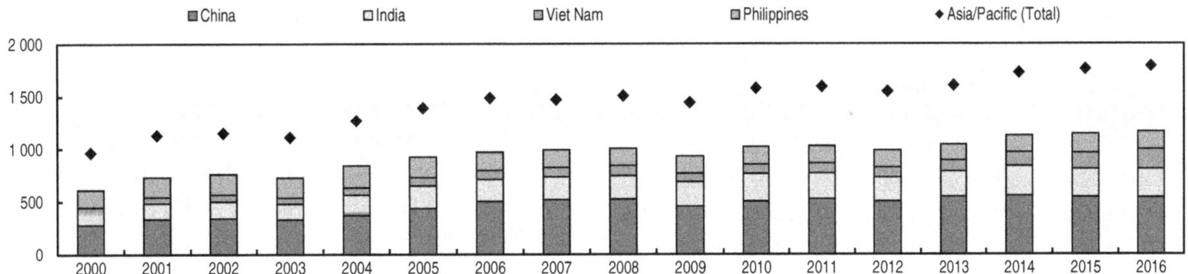

Note: 33 Asia/Pacific countries are included. Korea DPR, Mongolia, Timor-Lester are excluded.

Source: Inflows of foreign population by nationality, OECD International Migration Database.

StatLink http://dx.doi.org/10.1787/888933899926

Figure 3.12. **Approximately two thirds of migration remittance flows in Asia/Pacific are destined to India, China, and Philippines after 2006**

Migrant remittance inflows to Asia/Pacific economies (USD billion)

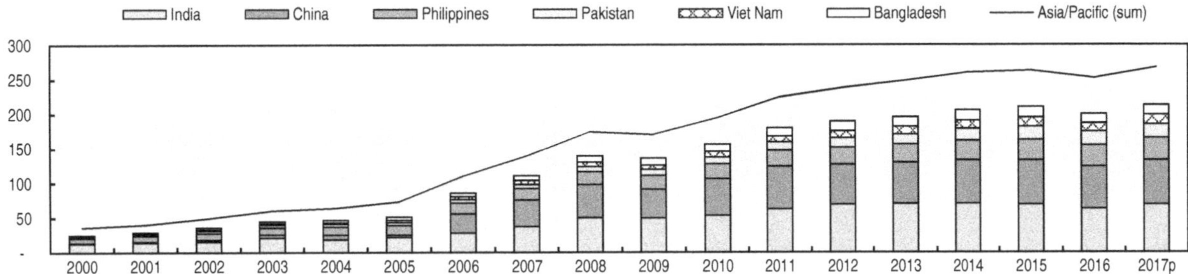

Note: 2017 data are estimates.

Source: World Bank Migration Remittances Data (April 2018 version).

StatLink http://dx.doi.org/10.1787/888933899945

OLD-AGE SUPPORT RATIO

In 2015, countries in the Asia/Pacific region on average had eleven people of working age for every person over 65 (Figure 3.13.A). This is more than twice as high as the OECD's average. Tajikistan, Maldives, Brunei Darussalam and Mongolia top the list with at least 17 working-age persons per one person of pension age: a stark contrast to Japan's 2:3 ratio. Within the Asia/Pacific region, OECD countries such as Korea, Japan, Australia and New Zealand have the smallest **old-age support ratios** compared with non-OECD countries. In these countries life expectancy is high (Figure 6.1), while fertility rates are low, particularly in Japan and Korea (Figure 3.4).

Old-age support ratios are projected to more than halve by 2055 (Figure 3.13.B), and the Maldives, Mongolia and Brunei Darussalam are expected to see the biggest declines. OECD Asia/Pacific countries already have low old-age support ratios and these will decline further, in particular in Korea, from over 5 in 2015 to around 1.5 persons of working age to 1 senior citizen in 2055. Although this decline is extremely rapid there are other economies in the region who will also experience rapidly ageing societies. For example, the old-age support ration in Viet Nam will decrease from 10.4 in 2015 to 2.5 in 2055. In China the old-age support ratio is projected to fall to a low level of 1.9 by 2055, just below the OECD average.

The upward trend in elderly population stems from a rise in life expectancy due to improved health and declining birth rates. Underlying **projected demographic trends do differ across countries** (Figure 3.14), but the proportion of people aged 65 and over is estimated to at least treble in most economies between 2015 and 2050. By 2050 it is estimated that at least 20% of the population win Asia/Pacific economies will be aged 65 or older. By 2050 over 36% of the population in Japan is estimated to 65 or older, the highest proportion of all countries in the region.

There are **economic and social implications** of demographic change. A low old-age support ratio provides some indication of the dependency burden on the working population, as it is assumed that the economically active proportion of the population will need to provide health, education, pension, and social security benefits for the inactive population, either directly through family support mechanisms or indirectly through taxation.

Data and measurement

The "old-age support ratio" relates the number of individuals aged 15 to 64 (working age) to the population aged 65 and over (those of "pension age"). All ratios are presented as the number of working age (15-64) people per one non-active person. The old-age support ratio thus provides a rough indicator of the number of active people who potentially are economically and socially supporting elderly people. It also gives a broad indication of the age structure of the population. Changes in the support ratio depend on mortality and fertility rates and, to a much lesser degree, on net migration.

Data come from the United Nations' World Population Prospects online database (2015, *http://esa.un.org/wpp/unpp/panel_population.htm*). The projections for population aged 65 used in this section are based on the "medium variant" population projections.

Figure 3.13. **Populations are ageing and the old-age support ratio will more than halve in the Asia Pacific**

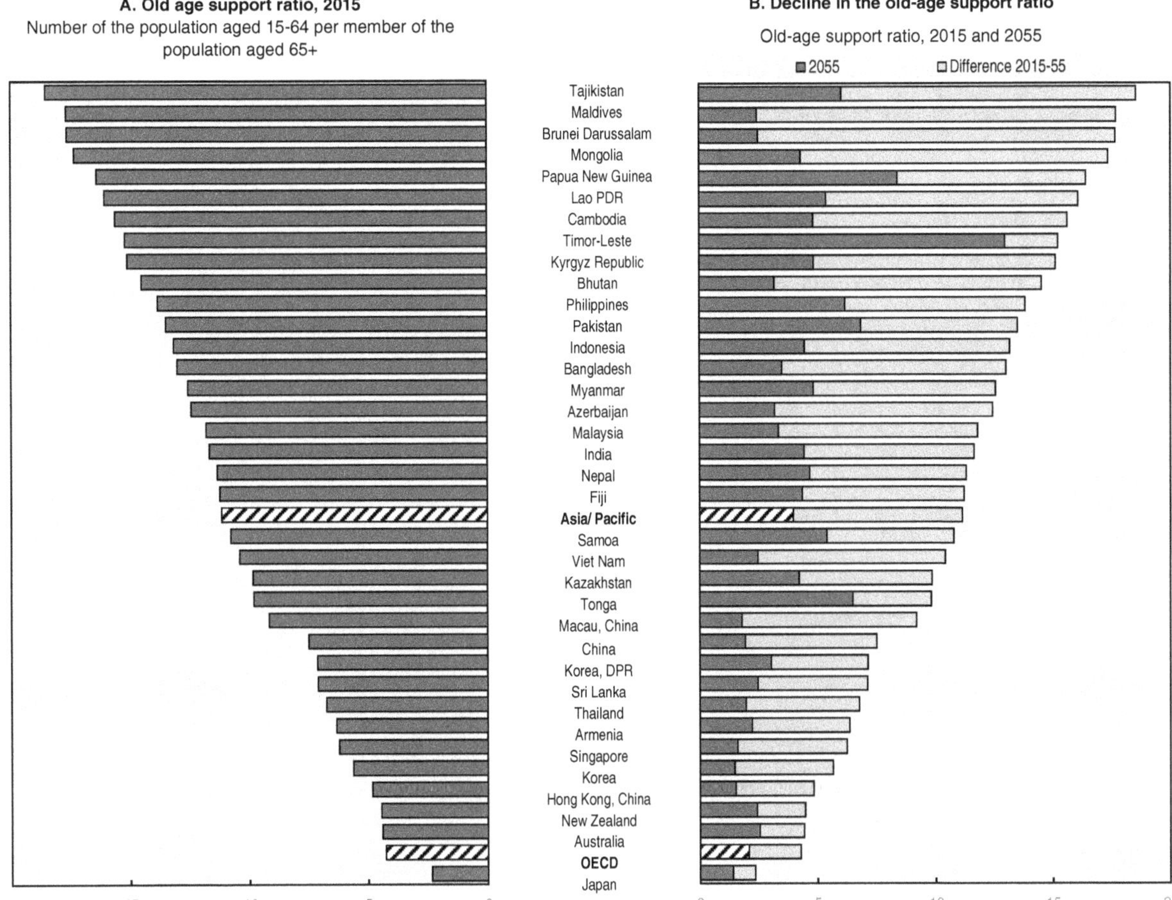

Note: The old-age support ratio is defined as the number of the population aged 15-64 per member of the population aged 65+.
Source: OECD Pensions at a Glance: Asia/Pacific 2018, UN World Population Prospects, 2015 Revision.

StatLink http://dx.doi.org/10.1787/888933899964

Figure 3.14. **Pensioner population projections**

Projected percentage of population aged 65 and over in selected countries, 2015-50

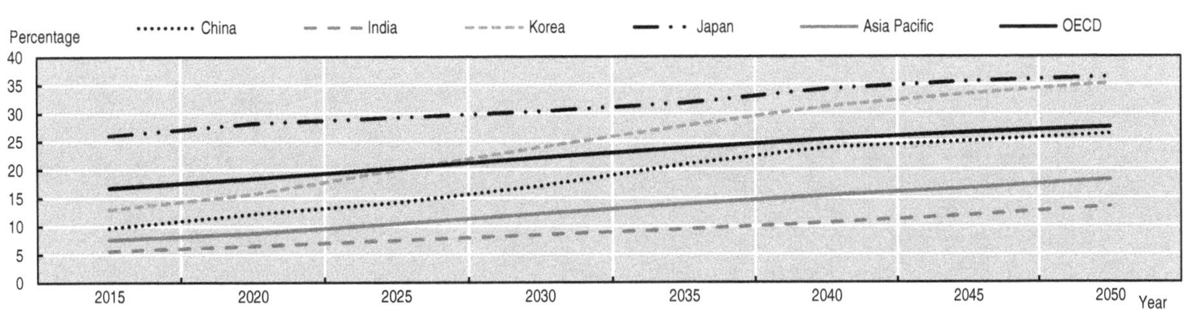

Note: The old-age support ratio is defined as the number of the population aged 15-64 per member of the population aged 65+.
Source: *OECD Pensions at a Glance: Asia/Pacific 2018*, UN World Population Prospects, 2015 Revision.

StatLink http://dx.doi.org/10.1787/888933899983

Society at a Glance
Asia/Pacific 2019
© OECD 2019

Chapter 4

Self-sufficiency

LABOUR FORCE PARTICIPATION

Labour force participation rates in 2017 were on average somewhat lower in Asia/Pacific economies (60.7) than in OECD countries (62.3), see Figure 4.1. In 2017, the highest labour force participation rates were recorded for China, Kazakhstan, Macau, New Zealand and Viet Nam at over 70%. The rates were below 55%, in India, Lao PDR, Pakistan, Samoa, Sri Lanka and Timor-Leste. Labour force participation rates are diverse across Asia/Pacific economies and by age group.

Considering **labour force participation rates by age**, in many Asian/Pacific countries labour force participation rates among older workers are relatively close to those for the total population, while rates for younger workers are significantly lower: on average across the region participation rates are 56% for older workers (55-64) and 41% for younger workers (15-24) in 2017. Exceptionally, younger workers in Cambodia and Myanmar have higher labour force participation rates than older workers.

Looking ahead, **OECD projections** show that – if male and female labour participation rates by five-year age groups follow the "baseline" scenario – the labour force will decrease by almost 10% by 2025 in Japan, with further declines anticipated up to 2040. Korea shows a similar patter after 2015 (Figure 4.2). By contrast, Australia, India, Indonesia and New Zealand are likely to see the size of the labour force increase over the next few decades. Assuming trends follow the baseline scenario, Australia, India and Indonesia could see the labour force grow by roughly 30% by 2040, and New Zealand sees increases of less than 20%.

G20 countries have committed to reduce the gender gap in labour force participation rates by **25% by 2025,** relative to the gender gap in labour force participation rates in 2012. This scenario would have a significant effect on the size of the labour force in several countries, especially India, where the labour force could potentially grow by another 138 million by 2040. Gains are likely to be smaller in **Australia, Japan and New Zealand**, largely because current trends are such that they are already expected to come close to the "25% by 2025" target under the baseline scenario (Figure 4.2).

Definition and measurement

The labour force participation rate is a measure of the proportion of a country's working-age population (15 and more) that engages actively in the labour market, either by working or looking for work for at least one hour in the reference week. It provides the relative size of the supply of labour available to engage in the production of goods and services. Data was taken from the ILO's Key Indicators of the Labour Market (KILM) database for non-OECD countries.

The labour force projections presented here are based on population projections for persons aged 15-74 years and current rates of labour market entry and exit. The model is a dynamic age-cohort model that projects future labour participation by gender and five-year age-group. Three scenarios are considered, and based on OECD population data and the OECD Employment Database.

1. Baseline: In many countries, there has been a trend increase in the participation of women which has offset a decline in participation rates for men, and there have been different trends by age. Rather than assuming fixed participation rates, the baseline scenario uses current (2007-16) rates of labour market entry and exit to project participation rates by gender and five-year age group over the period to 2040.

2. Gender gap reduced by 25% by 2025, and halved by 2040: Male participation rates are held at the baseline, and female participation rates projected so that the gender participation gap in 2025 is 25% smaller than the gap observed in 2012, and the gap in 2040 50% lower than in 2012.

3. Gender gap halved by 2025, and closed by 2040: Male participation rates are held at the baseline, and female participation rates projected so that the gender participation gap (within each five-year age group) in 2025 is 50% smaller than the gap observed in 2012, and by 2040 is closed completely.

Figure 4.1. **Labour force participation rates are diverse across Asia/Pacific economies and by age group**

Labour force participation by age group, 2017 or the earliest

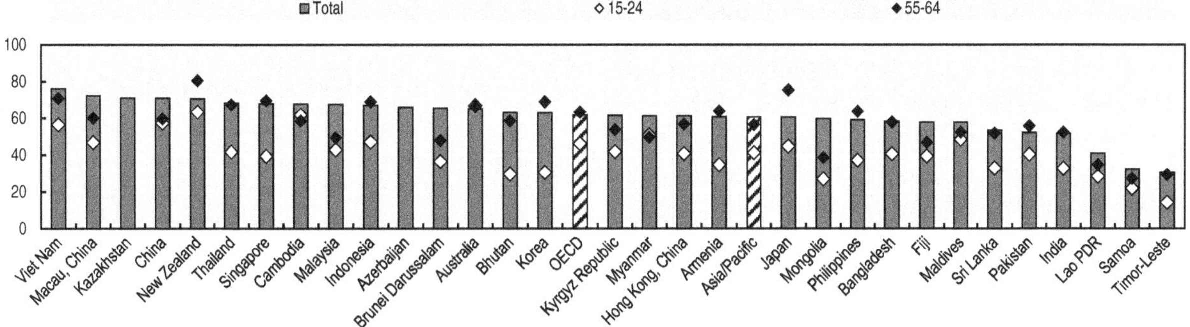

Source: ILO, Key Indicators of the Labour Market (KILM) and OECD Employment database.

StatLink http://dx.doi.org/10.1787/888933900002

Figure 4.2. **Labour force projections, selected countries, 2016-40**

Projected number of persons aged 15-74 in the labour force, thousands

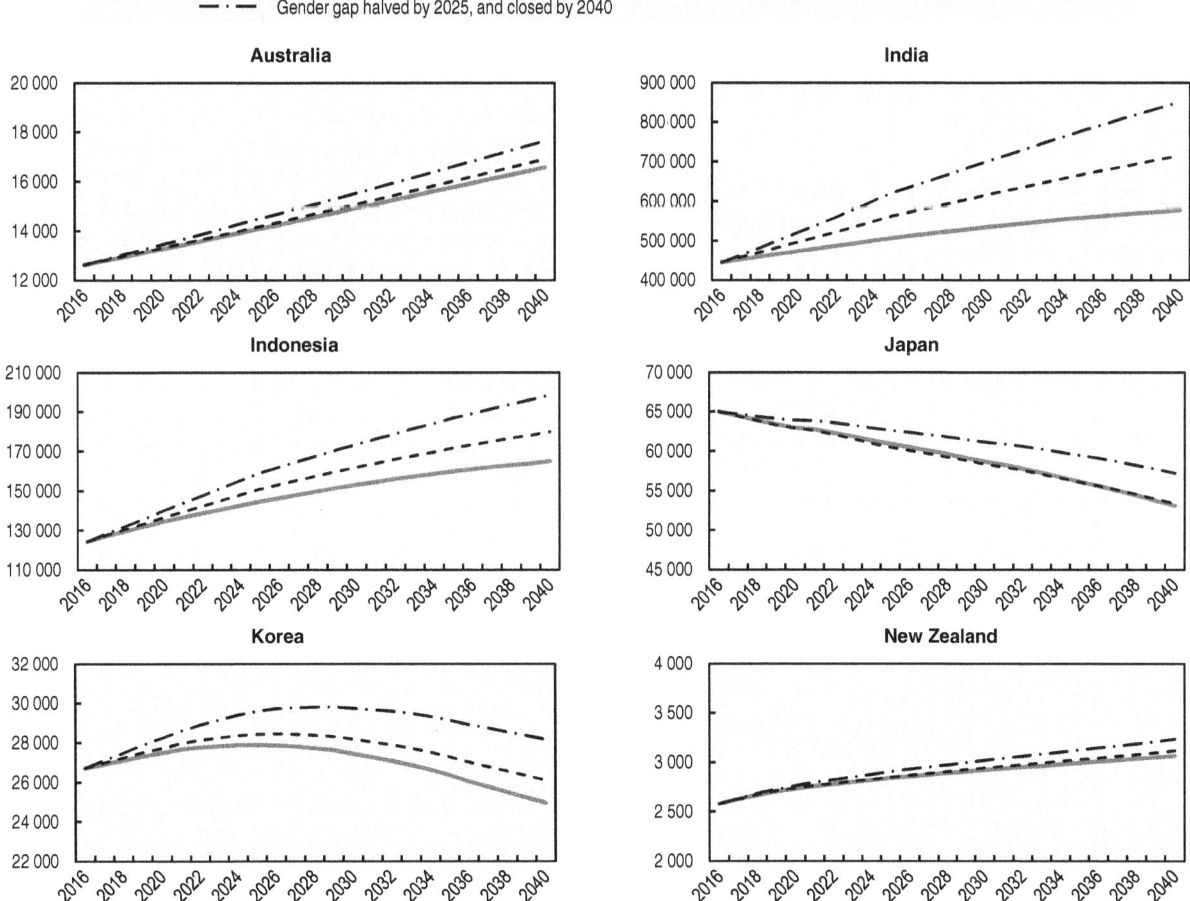

Note: The labour force projections are based on population projections for persons aged 15-64 years, by five-year age groups, and labour force participation data from the OECD Employment Database (www.oecd.org/employment/emp/onlineoecdemploymentdatabase.htm).

Source: ILO, Key Indicators of the Labour Market (KILM). OECD Secretariat calculations based on OECD population data and the OECD Employment Database (www.oecd.org/employment/emp/onlineoecdemploymentdatabase.htm).

StatLink http://dx.doi.org/10.1787/888933900021

EMPLOYMENT

Employment is a key factor in self-sufficiency. On average, about 60% of the population over age 15 were **employed** in Asia/Pacific and OECD economies (58.2%) in 2017 (Figure 4.3). A large disparity is observed: three in four of population over age 15 are employed in Nepal and Viet Nam, while only one in three have a job in Lao PDR, Samoa and Timor-Leste.

On average, as among OECD economies, employment rates in the Asia/Pacific region recovered close to pre- Great Recession levels in 2017, and employment is now higher than in 2007 in almost half of the Asia/Pacific countries. However, the employment rebound has been unequal across countries. The largest **increases in employment** between 2007 and 2017 – above 4.0 percentage points, were recorded for Malaysia, Singapore and Sri Lanka.

People in high-income economies are more likely to work in the **non-agricultural sector** compared with those in low-income economies (Figure 4.4). Over 80% of people employed in Brunei Darussalam, Hong Kong, China, and Singapore are engaged in the service-sector with less than 1% of all employed in the agricultural sector. By contrast, the largest share of employed people in Korea DPR and Nepal – over 67%, are in the agricultural sector.

Informal employment prevails in Asia/Pacific economies (Figure 4.5). Two out of three workers in the non-agricultural sector are engaged in informal employment in Cambodia, Bangladesh, India, Indonesia, Lao PDR, Myanmar, Nepal, Pakistan, Tajikistan and Timor-Leste. In contrast, informal employment only concerns one in six workers in Japan. Gender gaps in informal employment are small. Women in Korea, Lao PDR and Nepal are more likely to be in informal employment than men, but men are more likely to be involved in informal employment in countries that were part of the former Soviet Union, such as Armenia, the Kyrgyz Republic and Tajikistan.

Definition and measurement

The employment rate is defined as the ratio of employed people over age 15 to the population over age 15. Data was taken from the International Labour Organisation's Key Indicators of the Labour Market (LILM) Database for non-OECD countries and the OECD Employment Database for the Four OECD countries.

Employment by sector is based on the International Standard Industrial Classification of All Economic Activities (ISIC Revision 4). Data was taken from the International Labour Organisation's World Employment and Social Outlook – Trends 2018.

Informal employment is defined by the nature of the enterprise: own-account workers and employers are having the informal employment status when the job has the informal sector nature. Employers, with or without hired workers, operating an informal enterprise are classified as in informal employment. All family workers are classified as having informal employment, irrespective of whether they work in formal or informal sector enterprises (ILO 2018).

Figure note

ILO (2018), Women and men in the informal economy: A statistical picture (third edition), Geneva, *www.ilo.org/global/publications/books/WCMS_626831/lang--en/index.htm*.

Figure 4.3. **About 60% of the population over age 15 are employed in Asia/Pacific economies**

Share of employed people over age 15 to the population over age 15 (%), 2007 and 2017 or the latest year

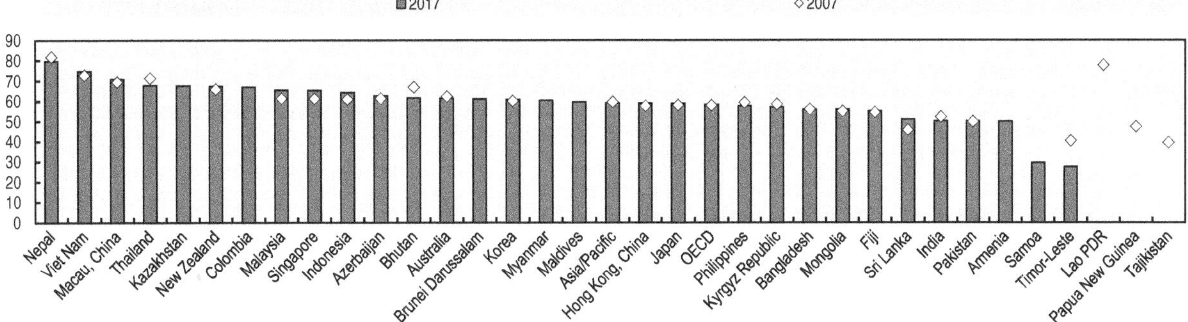

Source: Key Indicators of the Labour Market Database (ILO 2018) and OECD Employment Database.

StatLink http://dx.doi.org/10.1787/888933900040

Figure 4.4. **People in high-income economies are more likely to work in the non-agricultural sector**

Employment by sector, ILO modelled estimates (%), 2017

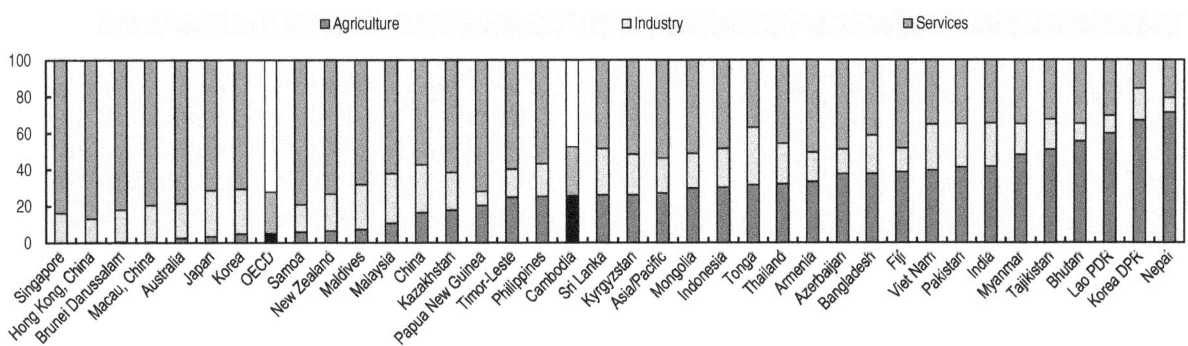

Source: ILO's World Employment and Social Outlook (ILO 2018).

StatLink http://dx.doi.org/10.1787/888933900059

Figure 4.5. **Informal employment prevails in Asia/Pacific economies**

Share of informal employment in total employment and in non-agricultural employment by sex (%), 2016 or the latest year

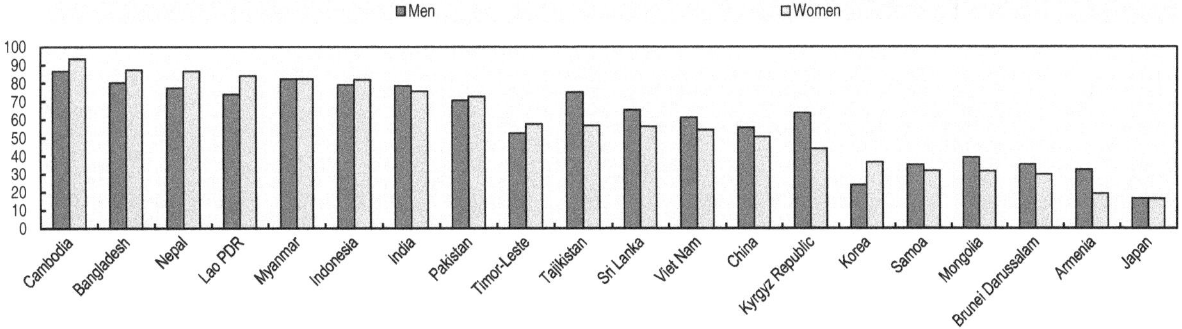

Source: Women and men in the informal economy: A statistical picture. Third edition (ILO 2018).

StatLink http://dx.doi.org/10.1787/888933900078

EARLY CHILDHOOD EDUCATION AND CARE

Public support for **early childhood education and care (ECEC)** services helps achieve a range of policy goals. Public investment in ECEC simultaneously enhances child development and helps children acquire the necessary skills to support their future lives, while it also supports parents in their daily quest to balance work and family commitments. As women traditionally engage most in care work, such supports particularly facilitate female labour force participation and are thus crucial to achieving greater gender equality in employment participation.

The extent to which **children participate** in pre-primary education (often children age 3-5 inclusive) varies across countries (Figure 4.6). Over the **2007-17 period** enrolment rates in pre-primary education in Asia/Pacific economies increased faster than the OECD average, where enrolment rates were already high in the mid-2000s. Pre-primary enrolment ratios tripled in the Kyrgyz Republic, Lao PDR and Samoa, and doubled in Myanmar, Mongolia and Philippines. **Gender gaps** in ECEC participation are small (Figure 4.7). Girls in Brunei Darussalam, Malaysia, Philippines and Samoa are more likely to receive ECEC services than boys, but boys are more likely to attend ECEC programmes in Macau, China, Nepal and Pakistan.

Results of the OECD Programme for International Student Assessment (PISA) have shown that fifteen-year-old students who had attended pre-primary education perform better on PISA tests than those who did not, even after accounting for their socio-economic backgrounds (OECD, 2011). For the few countries in the region for which data is available, higher rates of ECEC participation in 2005 are associated with higher score of the 2015 OECD PISA reading and mathematics assessment (Figure 4.8).

Definition and measurement

UNESCO data, **net enrolment rate for pre-primary**, are used for the early childhood education and care (ECEC) participation indicator. Net enrolment rate means total number of students in the theoretical age group for a given level of education enrolled in that level, expressed as a percentage of the total population in that age group. Therefore, the age of pupils participated in ECEC might differ across countries as targets and times of pre-primary education are not necessary same.

The Programme for International Student Assessment (PISA) is a triennial international survey which aims to evaluate education systems worldwide by **testing the skills and knowledge of 15-year-old students**. The data was taken from the OECD PISA 2015 Database.

The employment rate is defined as the ratio of employed people over age 15 to the population over age 15. Data was taken from the International Labour Organisation's *Key Indicators of the Labour Market (LILM) Database* for non-OECD countries and the OECD Employment Database for the Four OECD countries.

Further reading

OECD (2011), "Does participation in pre-primary education translate into better learning outcomes at school?", *PISA in Focus*, 1, OECD Programme for International Student Assessment, *www.oecd-ilibrary.org/education/does-participation-in-pre-primary-education-translate-into-better-learning-outcomes-at-school_5k9h362tpvxp-en*.

Figure 4.6. **Enrolment in pre-primary education in Asia/Pacific economies is increasing**

Net enrolment ratio of pre-primary education, total, %, 2007 and 2017 or the latest year

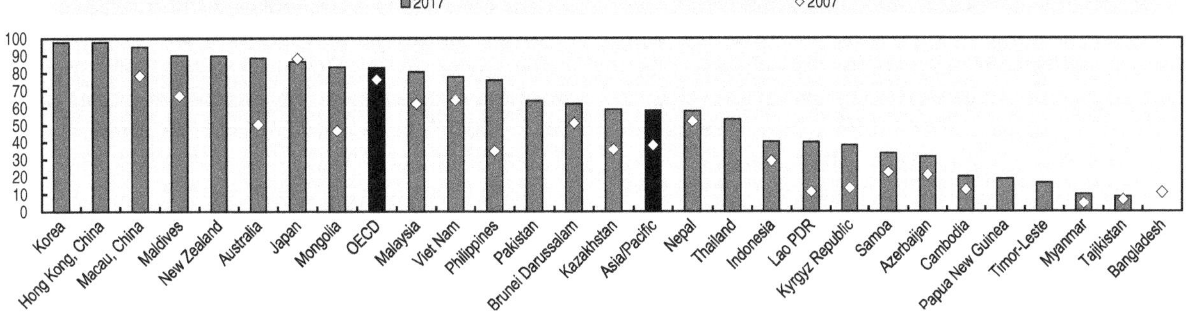

Source: UNESCO (2018), net enrolment ratios in pre-primary education.

StatLink http://dx.doi.org/10.1787/888933900097

Figure 4.7. **Gender gaps in pre-primary education participation are small**

Net enrolment ratio of pre-primary education, boys and girls, %, 2017 or the latest year

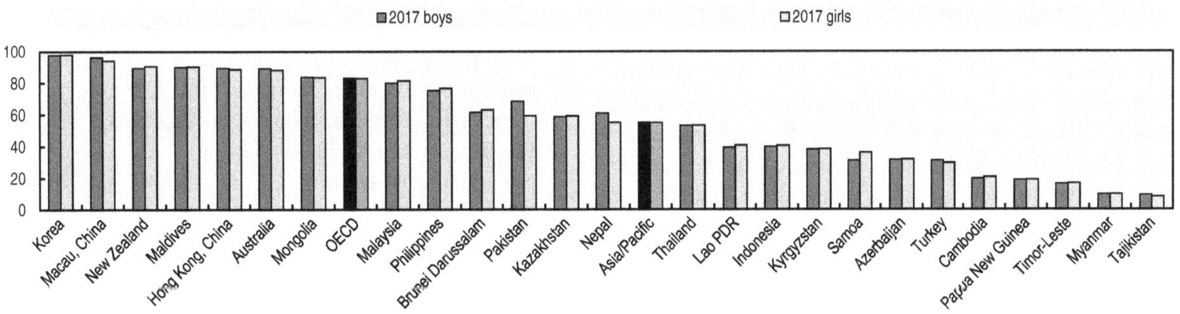

Source: UNESCO (2018), net enrolment ratios in pre-primary education.

StatLink http://dx.doi.org/10.1787/888933900116

Figure 4.8. **Higher rates of pre-primary education participation are associated with higher PISA scores**

Net enrolment ratio of pre-primary education of 2005 (%), total (X-axis) and the 2015 mean PISA score (Y-axis)

A. Reading Assessment

530 510 490 470 450 430 410 390 370 350

0 20 40 60 80 100

JPN, MAC, AUS, Asia/Pacific, VNM, OECD, KAZ, MYS, IDN

B. Mathematics assessment

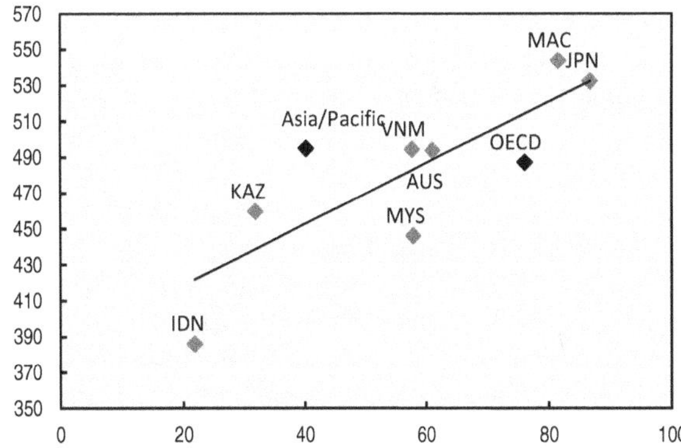

Source: UNESCO (2018), net enrolment ratios in pre-primary education; the OECD PISA 2015 Database.

StatLink http://dx.doi.org/10.1787/888933900135

EDUCATIONAL ATTAINMENT AND STUDENT PERFORMANCE

The **level of education** of the population gives an indication of its stock and quality of human resources. A higher stock and quality of human resources may mean higher labour productivity and hence a higher income-generating capacity. The average number of years spent in education among the working-age population is the most readily available and cross-nationally comparable measure of educational attainment across the Asia/Pacific region.

The United Nation Sustainable Development Goal 4.1 targets to ensure all girls and boys complete free, equitable and quality primary and secondary education (12 years) leading to relevant and effective outcomes by 2030. However, on average, the population over 25 years of age in Asia/Pacific economies has been in education for almost nine years with large cross-national differences (Figure 4.9). The population over 25 in Australia, Japan, and New Zealand spent more years in education than the OECD average (12 years), while in some countries – Bhutan, Cambodia, Myanmar, Lao PDR, Nepal, Papua New Guinea and Timor-Leste – the number of years spent in education is below five years on average. **Trends over the past decade**, suggest that the average years of schooling of those aged 25 and over increased across both OECD and Asia/Pacific economies (Figure 4.10), Especially, Indonesia, the Maldives, Nepal, and Singapore are rapidly increasing the average level of educational attainment.

There is a **gender gap in educational attainment** in Asia/Pacific economies in favour of men. Men over 25 in Asia/Pacific economies have spent on average 0.7 years more in education than women: this gender gap in mean years of schooling is significantly wider in Bhutan (2.1 years), India (3.4 years) and Nepal (2.8 years). Over the 2005-2017 period, many countries – China, Lao PDR, Malaysia, the Maldives and Singapore – have been closing the gender gap in mean years of schooling, while the gender gap increased in Bangladesh, Mongolia, Nepal, and Sri Lanka.

Future educational attainment levels in the Asia/Pacific region may well increase further relative to the OECD. Students from Singapore and large Chinese cities outscored students from OECD countries in mathematics and reading competency tests of the 2015 **OECD Programme for International Student Assessment (PISA)** (Figure 4.11). However, the performance of students in Indonesia, Kazakhstan, Malaysia, and Thailand was comparable with their peers in Colombia and Mexico, but lagged behind the OECD average.

Definition and measurement

Mean years of schooling measure average number of years of education received by people ages 25 and older, converted from education attainment levels using official durations of each level (UNDP 2018). Data on the average years of education is taken from Human Development Indices and Indicators based on UNESCO institute for Statistics (2018), Barro and Lee (2016), ICF Macro Demographic and Health surveys, UNICEF Multiple Indicator Cluster Surveys and OECD Education at a Glance(2017). The OECD programme for International Student Assessment (PISA) data was taken from the OECD PISA 2015 Database.

Figure note

UNESCO (2017), Unpacking Sustainable Development Goal 4 Education 2030 Guide, Paris, *http://unesdoc.unesco.org/images/0024/002463/246300E.pdf.*

UNDP (2018), Human Development Indices and Indicators 2018 Statistical Update, New York, United States, *http://hdr.undp.org/en/content/human-development-index-hdi.*

Figure 4.9. **On average those 25 years and older in the Asia/Pacific region have 9 years of school education**

Mean years of schooling, people aged 25 and older, 2017 or the most recent year available

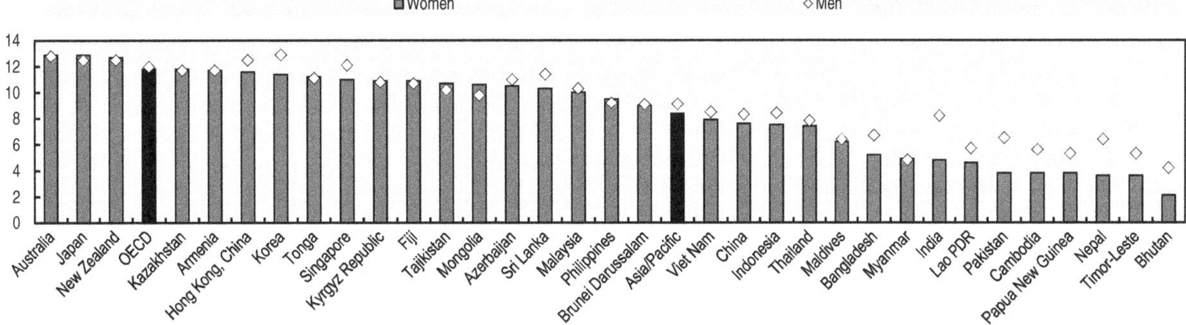

Source: UNDP (2018), Human Development data.

StatLink http://dx.doi.org/10.1787/888933900154

Figure 4.10. **The average years in schooling increased across the Asia/Pacific region over the past decade**

Change in mean years of total schooling (2005-17)

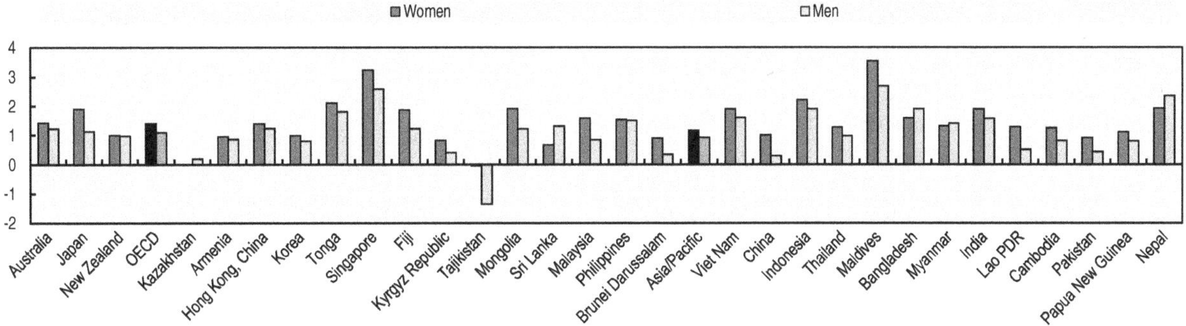

Source: UNDP (2018), Human Development data, Barro and Lee (2010).

StatLink http://dx.doi.org/10.1787/888933900173

Figure 4.11. **Students in the some Asia/Pacific cities outscored students from the OECD**

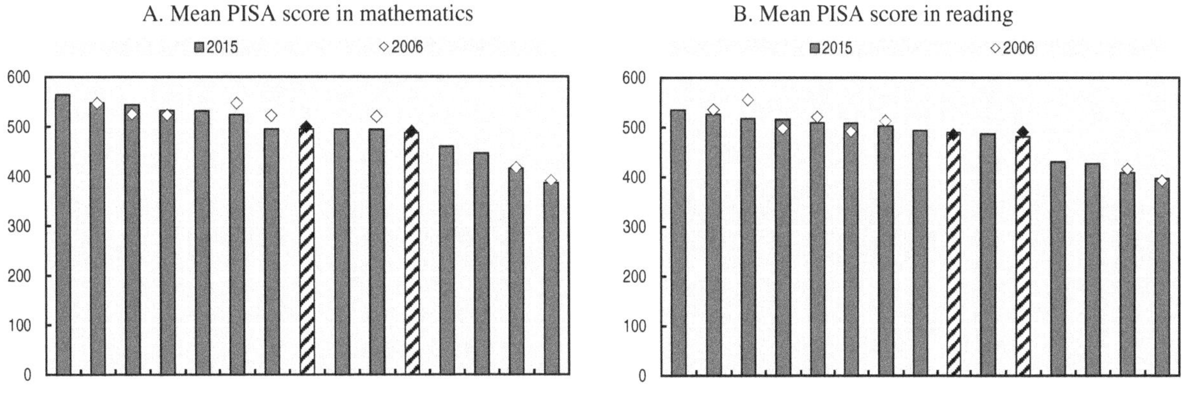

Note: B-S-J-G (China) refers to the four PISA participating China provinces: Beijing, Shanghai, Jiangsu, and Guangdong.

Source: OECD (2006, 2015), Program for International Student Assessment (PISA).

StatLink http://dx.doi.org/10.1787/888933900192

EDUCATION SPENDING

Public spending on education reflects **society's investment in children** to equip them with fundamental social and economic skills needed to be self-sufficient in life. Investing in education reduces poverty and boosts economic growth through human capital development, and is most efficient, in terms of long-term costs and benefits to society, and effective, in terms of human capital development, when investment starts during the early years and continues throughout childhood).

Public spending on education is around 4% of GDP on average across the Asia/Pacific and the OECD (Figure 4.12). However, cross-national variation is considerable: Public spending on education is over 7% of GDP in Bhutan and Kyrgyz Republic. By contrast, in Bangladesh and Cambodia public investment in education amounts to less than 2% of GDP.

On average across Asia/Pacific **public investment in education** in per cent of GDP increased since the mid-2000s. The increase in public spending on education as a per cent of GDP over this period was largest in Kyrgyz Republic and Brunei Darussalam (Figure 4.12, right scale). The largest decreases in the public education-to-GDP ratio (over 1 percentage point) were recorded for Fiji, Malaysia and Samoa.

Public spending on education as a percent of GDP can be higher in **richer countries** than in **poorer countries** but this is not necessarily so (Figure 4.13). For example, public spending on education as a per cent of GDP is similar in Australia, Korea, Mongolia, Samoa and Thailand, at very different levels of GDP per capita (Chapter 3). These differences can be explained by a range of factors, such as the role of private financing of education, which in Korea is among the highest in OECD countries, the level of wages of educators, costs of education material, and also population structures (Chapter 3). For example, the proportion of children (0-19) in the populations of Mongolia and Samoa (36% and 48% respectively) is much higher than in Australia (25%) or Korea (20%).

When considering **education spending per student** the picture is different. Public spending on education per primary student is higher in richer countries (Figure 4.14) in the OECD on average it is more than twice as high as on average across the Asia/Pacific region. Public investment in education per student in Nepal is comparatively low, but still higher than in Cambodia (KHM) where GDP is higher than in Nepal (Chapter 3).

Data and measurement

Data on public education spending as a per cent of GDP were taken from OECD (2018) Education at a Glance for the OECD, and the UNESCO Institute for Statistics for Asia and the Pacific (*http://stats.uis.unesco.org/unesco/ReportFolders/ReportFolders.aspx*). Public spending on education includes government spending on educational institutions including different levels of education as pre-primary, primary, secondary education and post-secondary education and tertiary education, spending on fee support for low-income parents and towards school meals is also included. Data on public spending per primary education student (in USD PPP) were taken from the UNESCO data centre (*http://data.uis.unesco.org/Index.aspx?queryid=191*).

Further reading

OECD (2018), *Education at a Glance 2018: OECD Indicators*, OECD Publishing, Paris, *www.oecd.org/education/education-at-a-glance/*.

United Nations (2017), "World Population Prospects – 2017 Revision", *http://esa.un.org/wpp/unpp/panel_population.htm*.

Figure 4.12. **Public investment in education increased across Asia Pacific countries**

Public expenditure on education as % of GDP

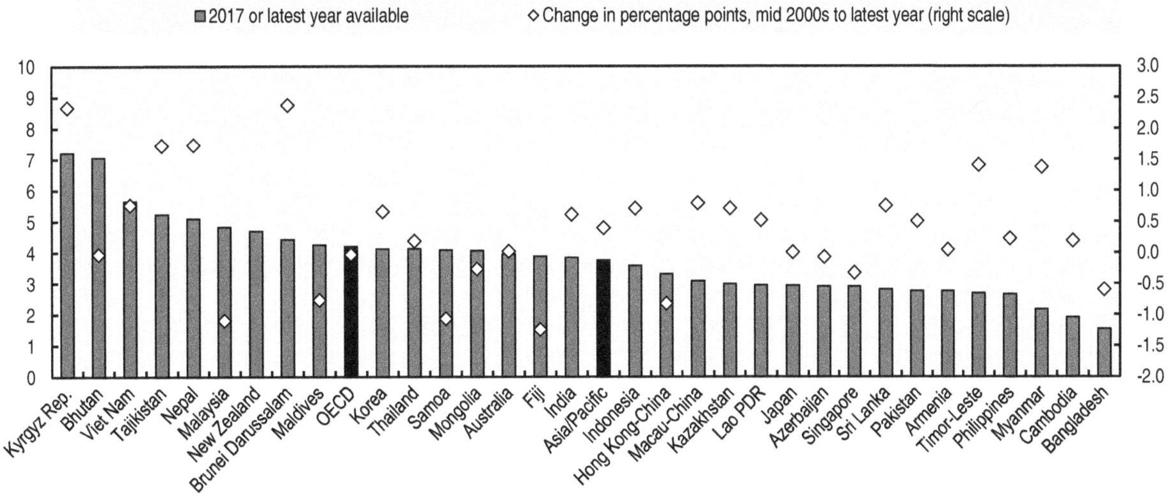

■ 2017 or latest year available ◇ Change in percentage points, mid 2000s to latest year (right scale)

Note: Data for change in the GDP share of spending on education, mid 2000s to latest year is not available for New Zealand.

Source: UNESCO Institute for Statistics, Finance Indicators by ISCED level, http://stats.uis.unesco.org/unesco/TableViewer/tableView.aspx?ReportId=172, OECD 2018 Education at a glance: Educational finance indicators, World Bank, World Development Indicators, http://data.worldbank.org/indicator.

StatLink http://dx.doi.org/10.1787/888933900211

Figure 4.13. **Rich countries do not necessary spend more on education**

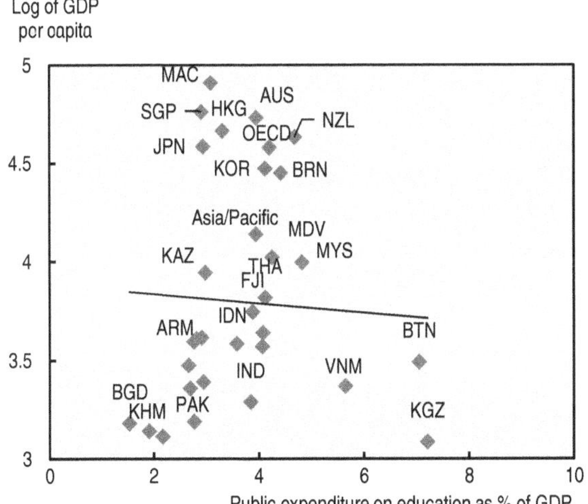

Source: UNESCO Institute for Statistics, Finance Indicators by ISCED level, http://stats.uis.unesco.org/unesco/TableViewer/tableView.aspx?ReportId=172, OECD 2018 Education at a glance: Educational finance indicators, World Bank, World Development Indicators, http://data.worldbank.org/indicator.

StatLink http://dx.doi.org/10.1787/888933900230

Figure 4.14. **Education as percentage of GDP and public spending per primary student**

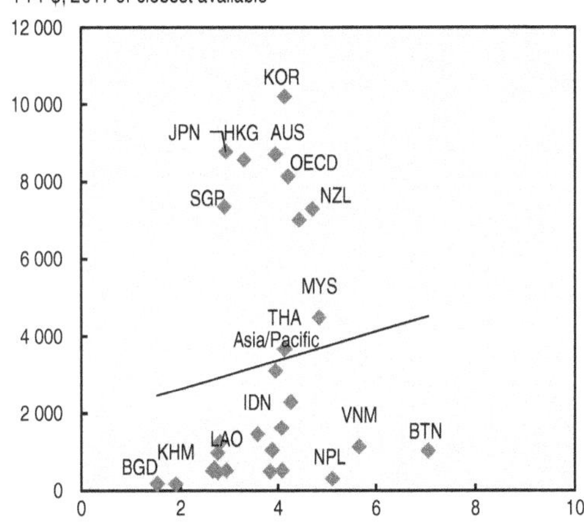

Source: UNESCO Institute for Statistics, Finance Indicators by ISCED level, http://stats.uis.unesco.org/unesco/TableViewer/tableView.aspx?ReportId=172, OECD 2018 Education at a glance: Educational finance indicators, World Bank, World Development Indicators, http://data.worldbank.org/indicator.

StatLink http://dx.doi.org/10.1787/888933900249

Society at a Glance
Asia/Pacific 2019
© OECD 2019

Chapter 5

Equity

POVERTY

There has been marked progress on **reducing extreme poverty** over last decade: the share of people living in extreme poverty – with incomes below USD 1.90 per day, has almost halved to 6.0% across the Asia/Pacific region (Figure 5.1). Much of the observed reduction was driven by remarkable progress in China, Indonesia, India, Timor-Leste, and Viet Nam, where poverty rates decreased by more than 16 percentage points.

Despite progress, **extreme poverty** is still **widespread** in India, Lao PDR, and Timor-Leste where more than 20% of the population have less to spend than USD 1.90 per day. Among low- and middle-income countries, poverty levels are lowest in China, Kazakhstan, Malaysia, Mongolia, Sri Lanka and Thailand where less than 1% of the population experiences severe poverty.

Poverty rates are a measure of inability to satisfy subsistence needs, including nutritional needs. The prevalence of **undernourishment** is generally correlated with the share of the population living under the USD 1.90 poverty line (Figure 5.2). However, in Sri Lanka and Tajikistan, the prevalence of undernourishment is well above what one would expect given poverty rates. Levels of undernourishment are also very high in Mongolia, Pakistan, Sri Lanka, Tajikistan and Timor-Leste. In these countries, social policies may take on a greater focus on food security.

Poverty generally **declined** more rapidly in countries with the strongest **GDP growth** (Figure 5.3). The pace of both economic growth and poverty reduction was fastest in Bhutan, China and Viet Nam over the 2006-16 period. In contrast, in Bangladesh and Lao PDR the share of population under the poverty line did not decline as much as what one would have expected given the pace of economic growth.

Definition and measurement

Poverty rates are commonly measured by using income or consumption levels. The poverty rate is a headcount of how many people fall below the poverty line. Extreme poverty is defined as living on less than USD 1.90 a day per person, measured in 2011 Purchasing Power Parity prices (World Bank 2018). The United Nation Sustainable Development Goal 1 aims to end poverty in all its forms everywhere by 2030.

The indicator also presents information on population below minimum level of dietary energy consumption, also referred to as prevalence of undernourishment, which shows the percentage of the population whose food intake is insufficient to meet dietary energy requirements continuously.

GDP per capita is calculated using a country's GDP in United States dollars (USD) which is then divided by the country's total population. Real annual average growth are calculated by using compound annual growth rate during the period (2006-16).

Further reading

World Bank (2018), Poverty and Shared Prosperity 2018: Piecing Together the Poverty Puzzle, Washington, DC, World Bank.

Figure 5.1. **The share of people living in extreme poverty has almost halved across Asia/Pacific during the last decade**

Percentage of population living with less than USD 1.90 per day, 2006 and 2017 or latest available

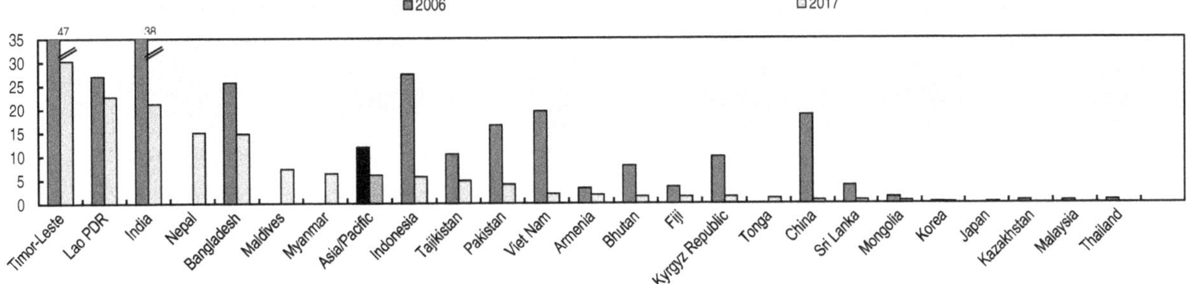

Source: World Bank, *World Development Indicators.*

StatLink http://dx.doi.org/10.1787/888933900268

Figure 5.2. **The prevalence of undernourishment is lowest in countries with a lower share of people living in extreme poverty**

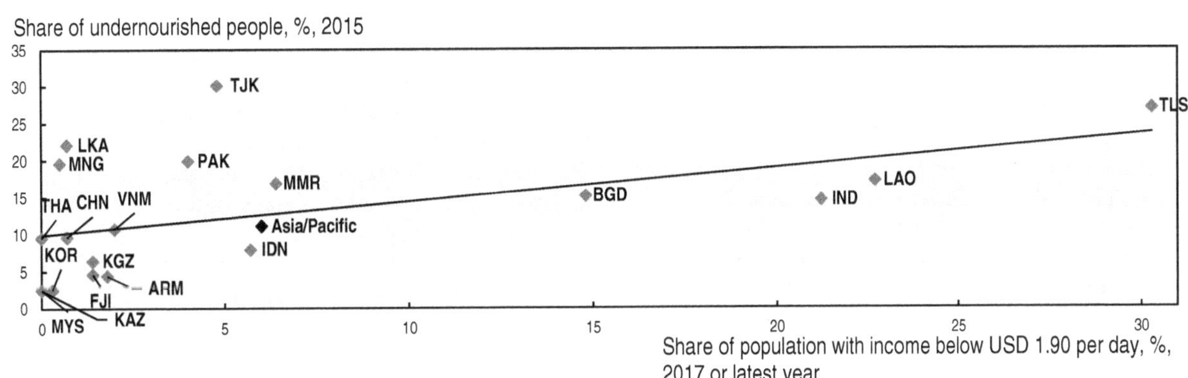

Source: World Bank, *World Development Indicators.*

StatLink http://dx.doi.org/10.1787/888933900287

Figure 5.3. **Poverty generally declined more rapidly in countries with strong GDP growth**

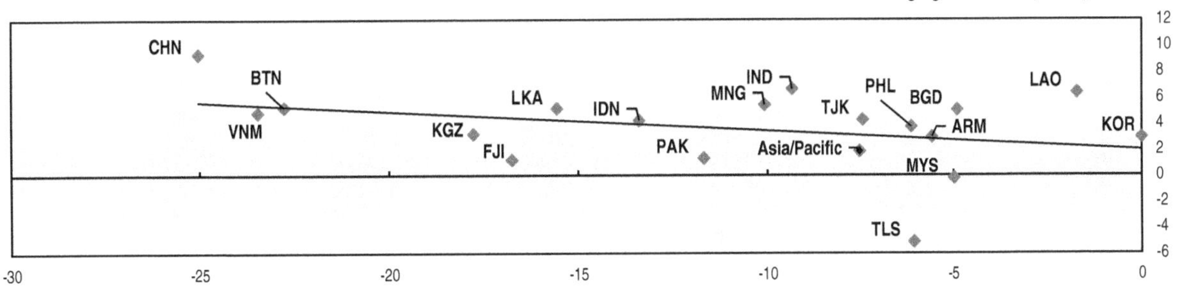

Source: World Bank, *World Development Indicators.*

StatLink http://dx.doi.org/10.1787/888933900306

INCOME INEQUALITY

Income inequality indicates how material **resources are distributed across society**. Some consider high levels of income inequality to be morally undesirable. Others believe that income inequality is bad because it causes conflict, limits co-operation or creates psychological and ultimately physical stresses. Often the policy concern is more for the direction of changes in inequality, rather than for its level.

Keeping measurement-related differences in mind, **income inequality** is high in the Asia/Pacific region compared to the OECD (Figure 5.4). In 2016, income inequalities were widest in Malaysia and China with Gini coefficients on income inequality at above 0.40, compared to around 0.25 in Kazakhstan and the Kyrgyz Republic. Over the past decade, income inequality across the Asia/Pacific economies remained around 0.35, which is above the OECD average (0.32). Some Asia/Pacific countries like the Fiji, the Kyrgyz Republic, Mongolia and Thailand experienced a reduction in income inequality over the past 10 years, while significant increases in income inequality were recorded in Armenia and Sri Lanka.

The **gap between** the average income and consumption of the **richest** and the **poorest** 10% of the population is similar in the Asia/Pacific economies and the OECD countries (Figure 5.5). The gap appears widest in Malaysia, and smallest in Kazakhstan and the Kyrgyz Republic. During the past decade, the gap declined in Bhutan, China, Fiji, Kazakhstan, the Kyrgyz Republic, Mongolia, and Thailand while it increased in Armenia, Lao PDR, Pakistan, Sri Lanka, Tajikistan and Viet Nam.

The relationship between income inequality and economic growth has stimulated much theoretical and empirical research over the past decades. But no consensus on the strength or even the sign of the **inequality-growth nexus** has yet been reached. There does not appear to be a clear country-correlation between economic growth and changes in inequalities among Asia/Pacific countries (Figure 5.6).

Definition and measurement

The main indicator of income distribution used is the Gini coefficient. Values of the Gini coefficient range from 0 in the case of "perfect equality" (each person receives the same income) and 1 in the case of "perfect inequality" (all income goes to the person with the highest income).

The indicator is the S90/S10 income decile share, corresponding to the gap between the mean incomes or consumption of the richest and the poorest 10% of the population.

OECD measures of inequality are based on income. For Asian developing countries, where most people are self-employed in agriculture or casual labourers, income data is often not relevant or non-existent. For most countries, inequality measures are expenditure-based. Thus country comparisons should be made with caution, as expenditure-based measures typically show lower inequality than do income-based measures. Data for non-OECD Asian countries are from the World Bank Development Research Group (*http://data.worldbank.org/indicator*) and data for OECD countries (based on equivalised disposable income) are from the OECD Income Distribution Database available at *www.oecd.org/social/income-distribution-database.htm*

Figure 5.4. **Income inequality of the Asia/Pacific remains higher than the OECD average**

Gini coefficient, 2008 and 2016 or latest year available

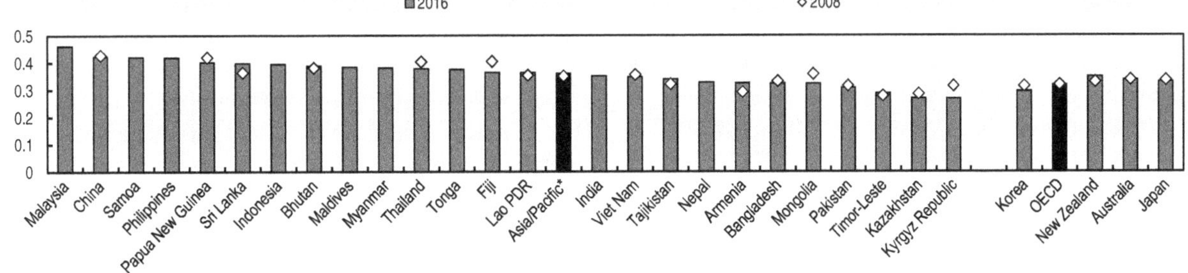

Note: The Asia/Pacific average does not include OECD four countries in this region.

Source: World Bank, *World Development Indicators*; *OECD Income Distribution Database* for OECD countries.

StatLink http://dx.doi.org/10.1787/888933900325

Figure 5.5. **S90/S10 income ratio in most Asia/Pacific economies declined over last decade**

Interdecile ratio S90/S10, 2008 and 2016 or latest year available

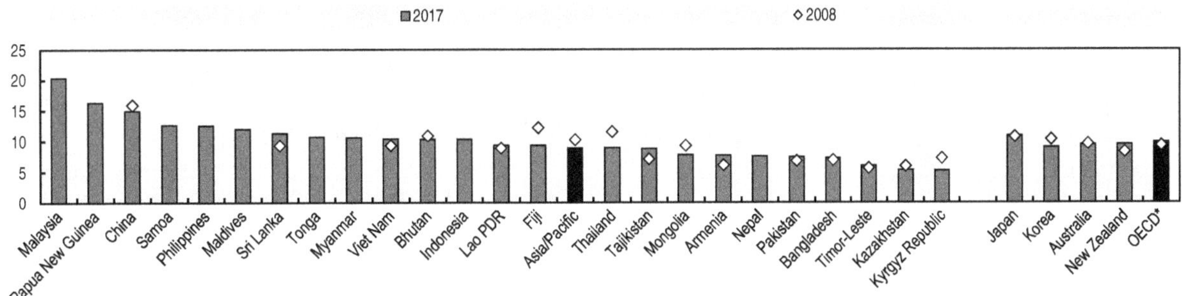

Note: The OECD average does not include Colombia.

Source: World Bank, *World Development Indicators*; *OECD Income Distribution Database* for OECD countries.

StatLink http://dx.doi.org/10.1787/888933900344

Figure 5.6. **Economic growth and income inequality seem unrelated**

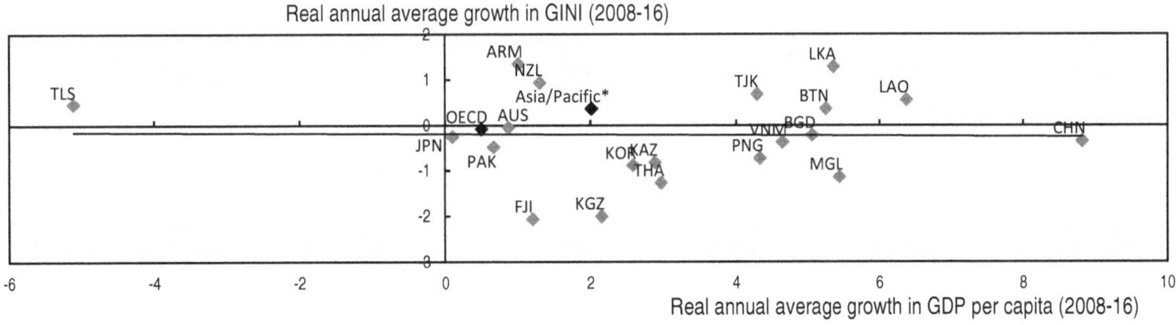

Source: World Bank, *World Development Indicators*; *OECD Income Distribution Database* for OECD countries.

StatLink http://dx.doi.org/10.1787/888933900363

PENSIONS: COVERAGE AND REPLACEMENT RATES

The proportion of people covered by a pension scheme and the extent to which pensions replace previous earnings are two important indicators of the role pension systems play in society. There is **huge variation of pension coverage** in the Asia/Pacific region (Figure 5.7): in Japan and Australia the pension system covers over 90% of the labour force while coverage is very low in Bangladesh, Cambodia and Lao PDR. One in three persons in the labour force and one in four people of working age are covered by mandatory pension schemes in the Asia/Pacific region, while this is 83% and 63%, respectively in OECD countries. There is a risk that the elderly in the Asia/Pacific region will have to rely more on family support to meet their needs than their peers in OECD countries.

In about half of the selected Asia/Pacific countries, the **redistributive nature** of pension systems leads to higher replacement rates for lower earners, which is likely to have a reducing effect on income inequality among older people. However, in India, Indonesia, Pakistan, Singapore, Sri Lanka, Thailand and Viet Nam, replacement rates are the same regardless of earning levels, and thus earnings inequality is "translated" into "pension inequality".

For **women** replacement rates are often below, or at best equal to, those for men without exception (Figure 5.8). In most OECD countries pensions systems as such do not lead to gender gaps in replacement rates. However in most non-OECD economies in the Asia/Pacific region generate lower replacement rates for women than for men. This is because in many countries women retire at an earlier age and so therefore have fewer years of contributions. Also women have a higher life expectancy and so for countries that have DC schemes – for which sex-specific life expectancy is used, they will receive less year on year. Alongside low pension coverage, the gender pension gap will be another factor to threaten the well-being of the elderly in Asia/Pacific economies in the future.

Countries with a lower GDP per capita have lower **pension coverage** (Figure 5.9). In low-income countries where the informal economy prevails, most people cannot afford or do not want to participate in mandatory pension schemes.

Definition and measurement

Pension coverage is defined as the proportion of people that are covered by mandatory pension schemes, and measured here by i) the population aged 15 to 64, and ii) the active labour force. The coverage value is expressed as the percentage of the population or labour force that is classified as active members of a mandatory pension system during the indicated year.

Often, the replacement rate is expressed as the ratio of the pension over the final earnings before retirement. However, the indicator used here shows the pension benefit as a share of individual lifetime average earnings (re-valued in line with economy-wide earnings growth). Under the baseline assumptions, workers earn the same percentage of economy-wide average earnings throughout their career. In this case, lifetime average re-valued earnings and individual final earnings are identical.

Figure 5.7. **There is huge variation of pension coverage in the Asia/Pacific region**

Coverage of mandatory pension systems, %, latest year available

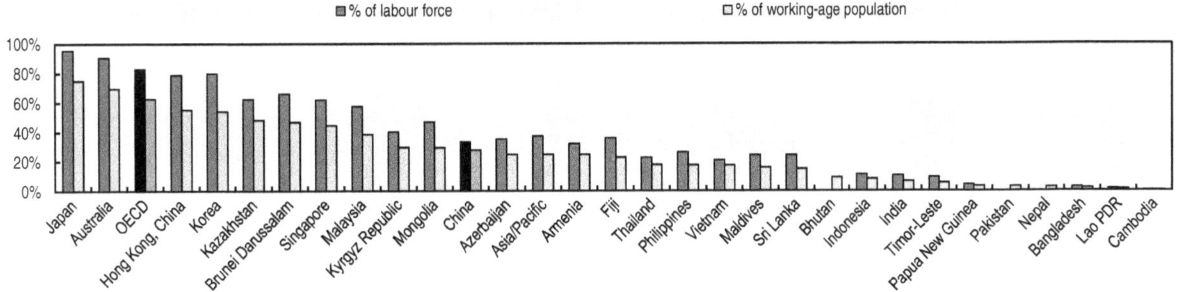

Source: World Bank (2018), *Pension beneficiaries coverage 3Q2014, www.worldbank.org/en/topic/socialprotection/brief/pensions-data.*

StatLink http://dx.doi.org/10.1787/888933900382

Figure 5.8. **For women replacement rates are below, or at best equal to, those for men**

Gross replacement rate, mandatory pension systems, latest year available

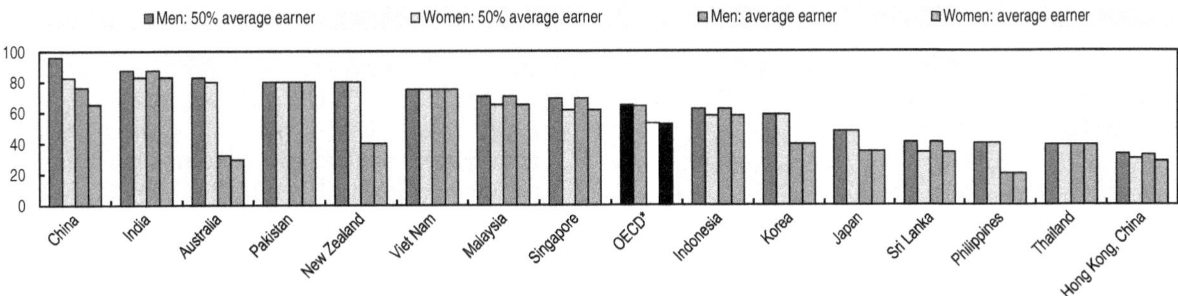

Note: OECD does not include Colombia and Lithuania.

Source: OECD Pension at a Glance: Asia/Pacific (2018).

StatLink http://dx.doi.org/10.1787/888933900401

Figure 5.9. **Countries with a lower GDP per capita have lower pension coverage**

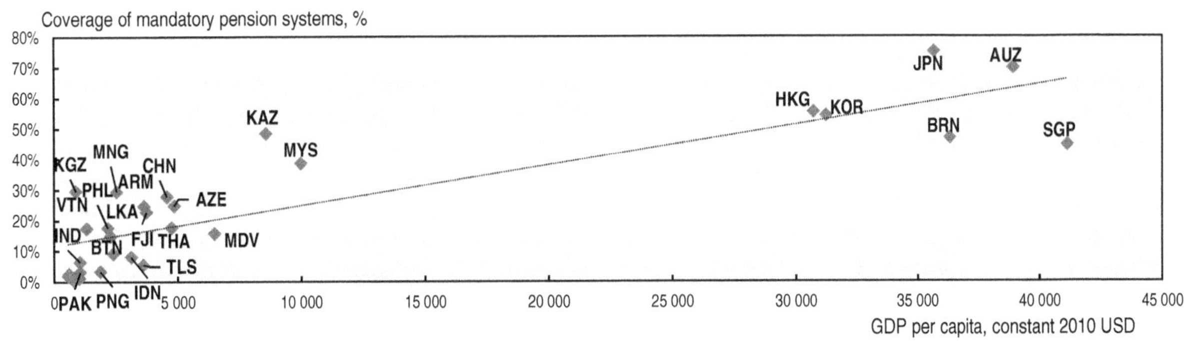

Source: World Bank, *World Development Indicators, http://data.worldbank.org/indicator.*

StatLink http://dx.doi.org/10.1787/888933900420

PUBLIC SOCIAL EXPENDITURE

In 2015, **public social expenditure-to-GDP ratios** varied considerably across the Asia/Pacific region, but were generally well below the OECD average (Figure 5.10). Average social protection spending in the Asia/Pacific region was about one-third of the average in the OECD as a whole. Public social spending in Japan, New Zealand and Australia is close to 20% of GDP, and around 10% of GDP in Korea, and Mongolia. By contrast, public spending on social protection is around 2% of GDP in Bangladesh, Cambodia, Lao PDR and Myanmar.

The **distribution of social spending** also varies across countries (Figure 5.11). On average, public spending on social insurance accounts for almost half of social spending; health expenditure account for more than one third; and, social assistance for about one fifth. However, there are large variations across countries: many Asia/Pacific economies have relatively young populations compared to OECD countries (see Figure 3.5), which helps to explain relatively small spending pension insurance benefits (Pensions: coverage and replacement rates).

In many Asia/Pacific countries, **social insurance** supports cover the relatively small public and formal sectors, and does not cover the large group of informal workers and/or self-employed workers and the elderly population who had little opportunity to contribute to pension schemes in the past. In all, social insurance benefits in many Asia/Pacific countries do not benefit the poor. Social insurance (which includes pensions) accounts for about 65% of reported social protection expenditure in Azerbaijan and Malaysia whereas it is less than 5% in Myanmar and Timor-Leste. Social Assistance (including assistance for elderly, child welfare, disability, welfare assistance) usually accounts for a relatively small share of reported social protection expenditure. Health accounts for more than two third of social expenditure in Myanmar, Bhutan, Cambodia, Papua New Guinea and Lao PDR whereas in Armenia and Azerbaijan only one fifth is dedicated to health related risks. Active labour market programmes play a relatively small role, except in Bangladesh where ALMPs account for around 15% of reported social protection expenditure (Figure 5.11).

Considering absolute poverty rates in low- and middle-income countries it appears that countries with **higher public social expenditure** tend to be those with **lower absolute poverty rates** (Figure 5.12). This suggests that public social spending helps to alleviate disadvantage and enhances equity.

Data and measurement

Public social expenditure concerns the provision of cash, in-kind and fiscal support to households and individuals. To be included in social spending, programmes have to involve compulsion in participation or interpersonal redistribution of resources, and address one or more contingencies, such as low income, old age, unemployment or disability. Social spending is public when general government controls the relevant financial flows.

Data on social protection for OECD countries were taken from the *OECD Social Expenditure Database* (SOCX). Public social spending for Asia/Pacific countries as in Figure 5.8, from the Asian Development Bank's Social Protection Indicator, as cleaned for partial health data, and include general government expenditure on health as taken from the WHO (World Health Organisation) Global Health Expenditure Database. Data for OECD countries are taken from the OECD Social Expenditure Database (SOCX). For Kazakhstan, Hong Kong, China and India data were taken from the ILO World Social Protection Report 2017-2019.

Public spending on education is not regarded as within the social domain, and spending data are generally not included here. Measurement issues affect the recording of data on public social protection expenditure, in particular regional/local social spending programmes are not always reflected in the available statistics for a country, e.g. as for India, and the data here may therefore underestimate public social effort. Social expenditure data coverage may differ between ADB, ILO and OECD, in term of countries and broad policy area, and therefore reported aggregate (regional) indicators of social spending by the different organisations are not the same. For data on poverty see indicator Poverty.

Figure 5.10. **Public social expenditure across the Asia/Pacific region are generally well below the OECD average**

Public social protection expenditure as a % GDP, 2015/17 or latest year available

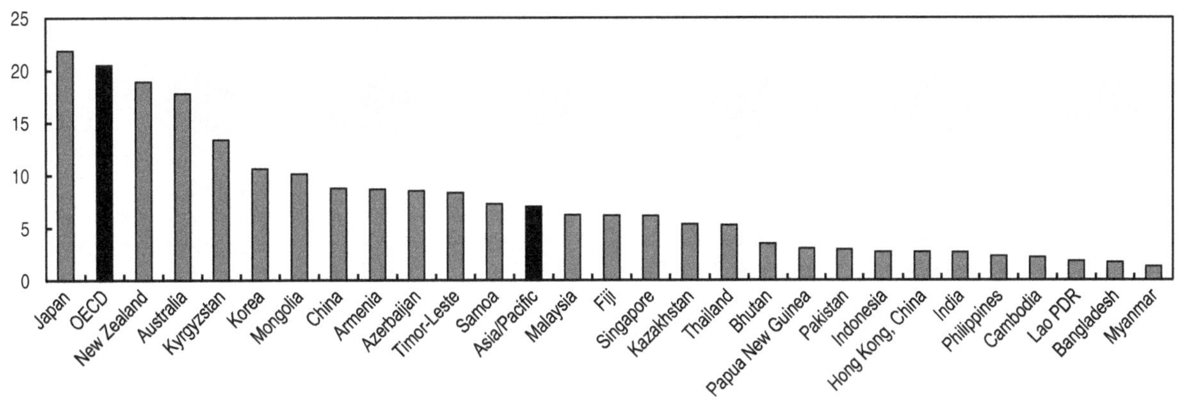

Source: OECD estimates based on ADB (2019), "The Social Protection Indicator: Results for Asia in 2015 (*http://spi.adb.org/spidmz/index.jsp – http://spi.adb.org/*); WHO (World Health Organisation) *Global Health Expenditure Database*, *http://apps.who.int/nha/database/ViewData/Indicators/en*; ILO World Social Protection Report 2017-19, *www.social-protection.org/gimi/gess/ShowTheme.action?th.themeId=3985*; OECD *Social Expenditure Database* (SOCX), (*www.oecd.org/social/expenditure.htm*); and, World Bank, *World Development Indicators*, *http://data.worldbank.org/indicator.*

StatLink http://dx.doi.org/10.1787/888933900439

Figure 5.11. **Social spending distribution varies across countries**

Public social protection expenditure by broad programme area, % GDP

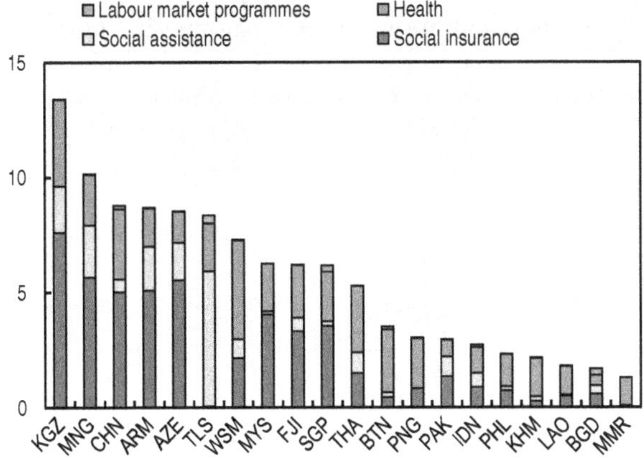

Source: See Figure 5.10.

StatLink http://dx.doi.org/10.1787/888933900458

Figure 5.12. **Public social spending and poverty**

Share of population living with less tha USD 1.9 per day, 2017 or latest

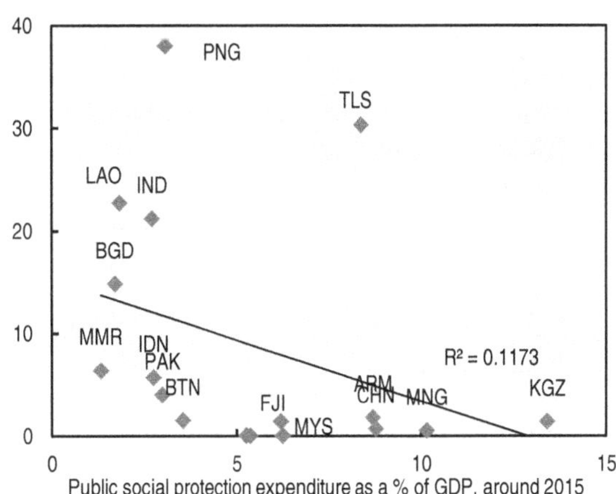

Source: See Figure 5.10.

StatLink http://dx.doi.org/10.1787/888933900477

SOLIDARITY

Making donations to charities, doing voluntary work or helping strangers are all examples of **showing compassion** to others, contribute to the functioning of society and/or supporting the disadvantaged. Income levels can to some extent explain observed differences between countries, but different traditions regarding the supportive role of the state, the community and the family are also important.

On average, people living in OECD countries are slightly more likely to make **donations to charities** than people across the Asia/Pacific region (Figure 5.13). However, while the incidence of donating to charities increased slightly across the Asia/Pacific region it declined somewhat across the OECD. (Figure 5.13). Among OECD countries people in Australia and New Zealand are twice as likely to donate to charity as people in Japan and Korea. People in Indonesia and Thailand are also more likely to make donations to charity than elsewhere across the Asia/Pacific region, and the likelihood that Indonesians, Kazakhs and Kyrgyzs give to charity has increased in recent years.

Alternative ways of showing solidarity can be through helping a stranger or offering time to an organisation or charity. In recent years, the share of people who **helped a stranger** increased marginally on average across the Asia/Pacific region and OECD countries (Figure 5.14). Pakistan and Singapore had the largest increase in altruistic behaviour towards strangers over the past decade, while Australians and New Zealanders appear to be the most likely to help a stranger in need.

The share of people who **volunteered time** is pretty stable in the OECD and Asia/Pacific region (Figure 5.15). On average, one in four people volunteered time to an organisation. Across 2015-17. Indonesia had the highest number of volunteers, showing a large increase since 2006-08. By contrast, less than 10% of the population in Armenia, Cambodia and China made time available for charitable work.

Data and measurement

Data on "solidarity" are drawn from the Gallup World Poll. The Gallup World Poll is conducted in more than 150 countries around the world based on a common questionnaire, translated into the predominant languages of each country. With few exceptions, all samples are probability based and nationally representative of the resident population aged 15 years and over in the entire country, including rural areas. While this ensures a high degree of comparability across countries, results may be affected by sampling and non-sampling error, and variation in response rates. Hence, results should be interpreted with care. These probability surveys are valid within a statistical margin of error, also called a 95% confidence interval. This means that if the survey is conducted 100 times using the exact same procedures, the margin of error would include the "true value" in 95 out of 100 surveys. Sample sizes vary across countries from 1 000 to 4 000, and as the surveys use a clustered sample design the margin of error varies by question. The margin of error declines with increasing sample size: with a sample size of 1 000, the margin of error at a 95% confidence interval is $0.98/\sqrt{\text{sample size}}$ or 3%; with a sample size of 4 000, this is 1.5%. To minimise the effect of annual fluctuations in responses related to small sample sizes, results are averaged over a three-year period, or two-year period in case of missing data. If only one observation in a three-year period is available this finding is not reported.

The data underlying the solidarity indicators are based on binary questions created by Gallup: "Have you done any of the following in the past month? How about donating money to a charity? How about helped a stranger or someone you didn't know who needed help? How about volunteering your time to an organisation?" There are no questions about the amount of money donated of number of hours volunteered.

Figure 5.13. **The propensity to give to charity varies widely across Asia/Pacific countries**

Share of people who have donated money to a charity in the last month (%)

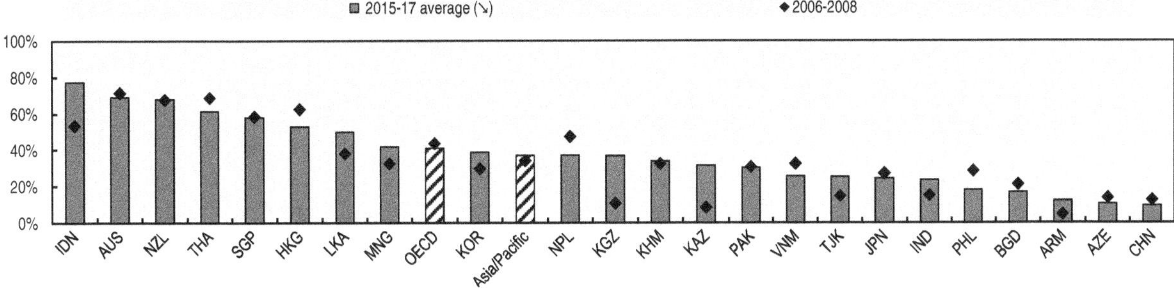

Note: Percentage point change between 2006-08 and 2015-17 is not available for Bangladesh and Pakistan.
Source: Gallup World Poll, *www.gallup.com*.

StatLink http://dx.doi.org/10.1787/888933900496

Figure 5.14. **The share of people who helped a stranger increased slightly in the Asia/Pacific**

Share of people who helped a stranger or someone they didn't know who needed help in the past month (%)

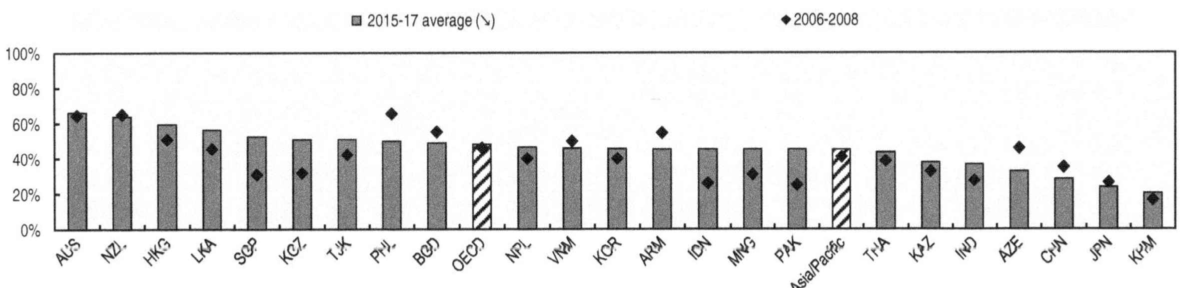

Source: Gallup World Poll, *www.gallup.com*.

StatLink http://dx.doi.org/10.1787/888933900515

Figure 5.15. **On average, one in four people volunteers time to an organisation across OECD and Asia/Pacific**

Share of people who volunteered time to an organization in the past month (%)

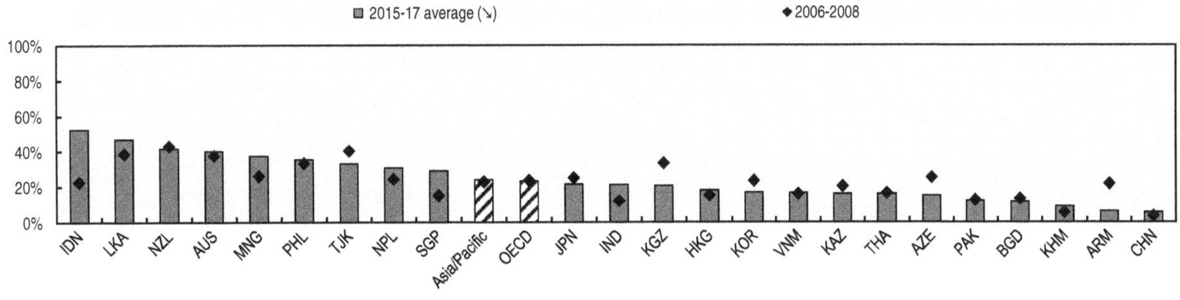

Source: Gallup World Poll, *www.gallup.com*.

StatLink http://dx.doi.org/10.1787/888933900534

Figure 5.13. The propensity to give to charity varies widely across Asia/Pacific countries

Figure 5.14. The share of people who helped a stranger increased significantly in the Asia/Pacific

Society at a Glance
Asia/Pacific 2019
© OECD 2019

Chapter 6

Health

LIFE EXPECTANCY

Life expectancy at birth is a general measure of a population's health status, and is often used to gauge the development of a country's health. **Life expectancy at birth continues to rise** in Asia and the Pacific, averaging about 74.2 years in 2016 up from 69.4 years in 2000 (Figure 6.1). Since 2000 the largest increases in life expectancy were recorded for Cambodia (11.7 years), Lao PDR, and Nepal (7.7 years). This rapid growth is related to a number of factors, including rising living standards, better nutrition, water and sanitation, increased education and greater access to health services. Nevertheless, despite the significant increase, life expectancy in the Asia/Pacific still lags behind other world regions except Africa (UN World Population Prospects data, 2017).

There is large **cross-national variation** in life expectancy across the region: life expectancy at birth is 80 years or more in East Asia, while this is 70 years or less in some Southern and South-Eastern Asian countries (Cambodia, Indonesia, Myanmar and the Philippines) as well as the island nations of Papua New Guinea and Fiji. On average in the Asia/Pacific region **women outlive men** by almost five years. Women in China, Fiji and Mongolia, outlive men by seven years or more, while this is just over one or two year in Brunei Darussalam and Pakistan. Women in Hong Kong (China) and Japan, have the highest life expectancy at birth at over 86 years compared to 81 years for men.

More and more people in Asia become **senior citizens**. About 90% of population reach the age of 65 in Australia, Japan, Hong Kong, China, Korea, Macau, China, New Zealand and Singapore (Figure 6.2). Men in Mongolia and Myanmar and men and women in Papua New Guinea are least likely to become 65 years of age – less than 70% for women and 60% for men.

Although **higher national income**, measured by GDP per capita, is generally associated with **longer life expectancy** at birth, this does not always hold. Viet Nam has one of the lowest incomes per capita in the region at about USD 6 300, but has a relatively high life expectancy at 86 years on average, by contrast, Brunei Darussalam has a GDP per capita of USD 77 400 and a life expectancy of 76 years on average (Figure 6.3).

Definition and measurement

Life expectancy measures how long, on average, a new-born infant would live if the prevailing patterns of mortality at the time of birth were to stay the same throughout their lifetime. Since the factors that affect life expectancy do not change overnight, variations are best assessed over long periods of time. Countries calculate life expectancy according to methodologies that can vary somewhat, and these can lead to differences of fractions of a year. Some countries base their life expectancies on estimates derived from censuses and surveys, and not on the accurate registration of deaths.

Survival rate to age 65 refers to the percentage of a cohort of new-born infants that would survive to age 65, if subject to current age-specific mortality rates.

Figure 6.1. **Life expectancy at birth continues to rise in the Asia/Pacific region**

Life expectancy at birth, by sex, 2000 and 2016

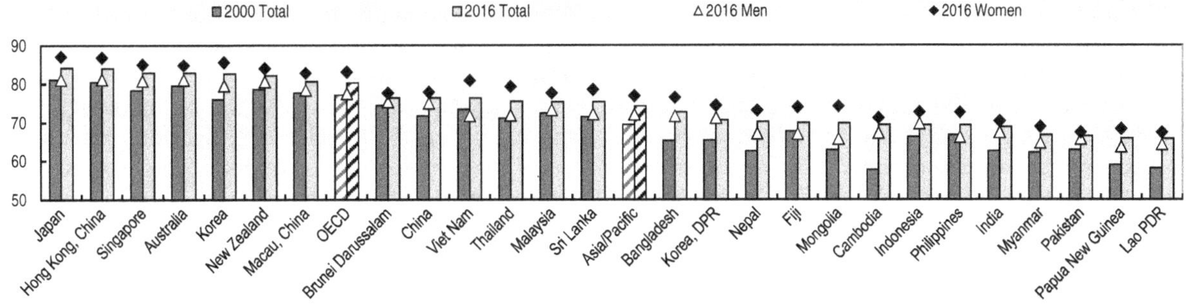

Source: OECD Health Statistics 2016; WHO; World Bank, *World Development Indicators*.

StatLink http://dx.doi.org/10.1787/888933900553

Figure 6.2. **More and more people, in Asia reach the age of 65**

Survival rate to age 65, by sex, 2016

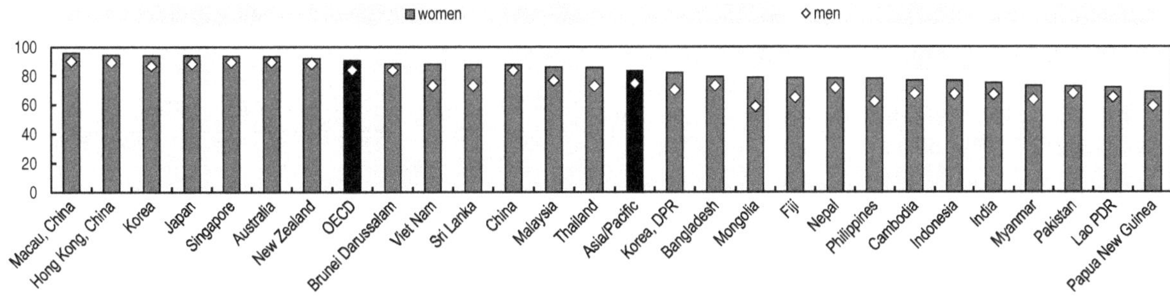

Source: World Bank, *World Development Indicators*.

StatLink http://dx.doi.org/10.1787/888933900572

Figure 6.3. **Higher national income (as measured by GDP per capita) is generally associated with higher life expectancy at birth**

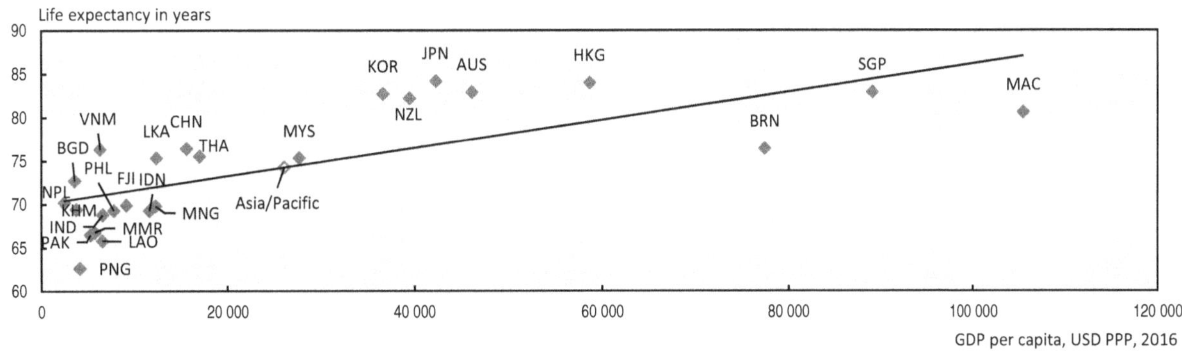

Source: OECD Health Statistics 2016; World Bank, *World Development Indicators*.

StatLink http://dx.doi.org/10.1787/888933900591

INFANT AND CHILD MORTALITY

Infant mortality – death among children not yet one year of age, reflects the effect of economic, social and environmental conditions on the **health of mothers and infants**, as well as the effectiveness of health systems. Child mortality – death among children not yet 5 years of age an indicator of **child health** as well as the overall development and well-being of a population. As part of their Sustainable Development Goals, the United Nations has set a target of reducing under age 5 mortality to at least as low as 25 per 1 000 live births by 2030 (United Nations 2015).

Over the 2000-16 period, **infant mortality rates** have roughly **halved** in the Asia/Pacific region, but huge **cross-national disparities** exists across countries. Advanced economies have the lowest infant mortality rates, often lower than OECD average (4.0): Macau, China, Hong Kong, China, Japan, and Singapore record infant mortality rates of around two deaths per 1 000 live births (Figure 6.4). In contrast, low-income countries such as Lao PDR, Myanmar, Papua New Guinea, Pakistan and Timor-Leste have infant mortality rates exceeding 40 deaths per 1 000 live births.

Across the selected countries, the highest incidence of infant mortality is recorded for children with mothers who low **educational attainment** and little **income** who live in rural areas (Figure 6.5). While all the selected countries show similar trends, the infant mortality discrepancies upon socio-economic status of mothers were widest in Lao DPR (2011-12): the infant mortality rate was 95 among low-income wealth families and 27 for high-income families; 96 for mothers with low educational attainment and 32 for mothers with high educational attainment; and, 85 for mothers in rural areas and 39 for mothers in urban areas.

Child mortality rates have halved over the 2000-16 period. However, one-third of Asia/Pacific countries have not yet achieved the Sustainable Development Goal of a child mortality rate of 25 or less per 1 000 live births by 2030 (Figure 6.6). Lao PDR, Myanmar, Pakistan, and Papua New Guinea have child mortality rates exceeding 50 deaths per 1 000 live births though child mortality rates fell significantly over the past fifteen years. Boys are more likely than girls to die before their fifth birthday in all countries except Tonga, although the gender gap in child mortality has narrowed over the past fifteen years.

Definition and measurement

The infant mortality rate is defined as the number of children who die before reaching their first birthday in a given year, expressed per 1 000 live births. The child mortality rate (or under-five mortality rate – U5MR) is the probability – expressed as a rate per 1 000 live births, of a child born in a specified years dying before reaching the age of five when subject to current age-specific mortality rates.

Some countries base their infant mortality rates on estimates derived from censuses, surveys and sample registration systems, and not on accurate and complete registration of births and deaths. Differences among countries in registering practices for premature infants may also add slightly to international variations in rates.

Further reading

The UN inter-agency Group (UNICEF, WHO, World Bank Group, United Nations) for Child Mortality Estimation (2017), "Levels & Trends in Child Mortality", *www.unicef.org/publications/index_101071.html.*

Figure 6.4. **The infant mortality rate has halved, while huge disparities exist across countries**

Infant mortality rate, per 1 000 live births, 2000 and 2016

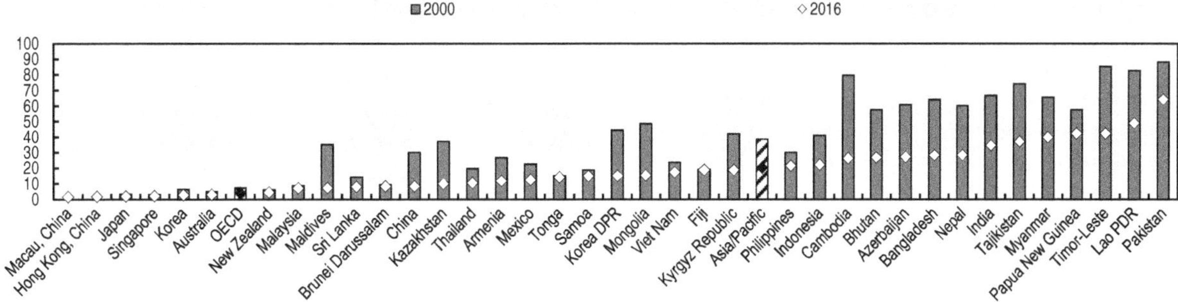

Source: UN Inter-agency Group for Child Mortality Estimation (IGME) Child Mortality Report 2017; Hong Kong annual digest of statistics 2017; Macau yearbook of Statistics, 2016.

StatLink http://dx.doi.org/10.1787/888933900610

Figure 6.5. **Mothers experienced high incidence of infant mortality when they have low education and wealth and live in rural areas**

Infant mortality rate by wealth, location, and mothers' education, selected countries and years

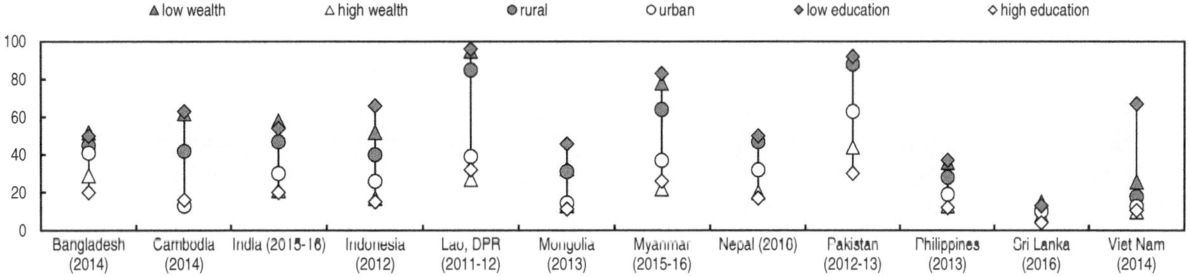

Source: Demographic and Health Survey (DHS) and Multiple Indicator Cluster Survey (MICS) 2012-16.

StatLink http://dx.doi.org/10.1787/888933900629

Figure 6.6. **The child mortality rate halved to 24.6 since 2000, but the gender gap still exists**

Child (under 5) mortality, per 1 000 live births, by sex, 2000 and 2016

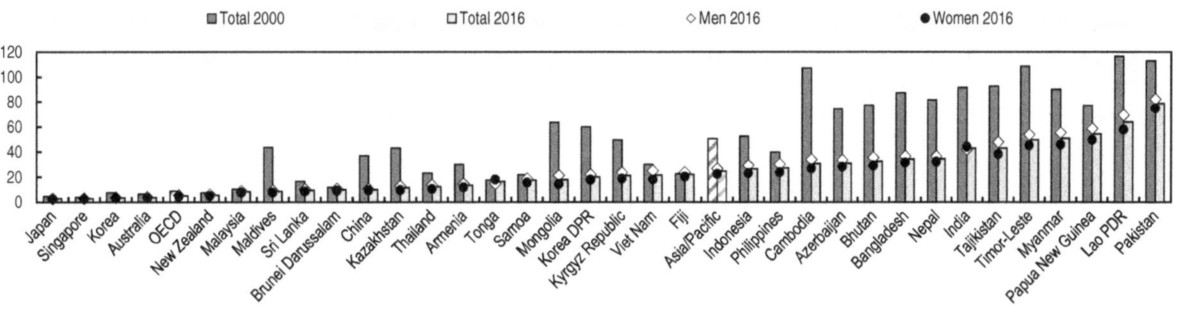

Source: WHO Global Health Observatory data (2018), UN Inter-agency Group for Child Mortality Estimation (IGME) Child Mortality Report 2017.

StatLink http://dx.doi.org/10.1787/888933900648

CHILD MALNUTRITION (INCLUDING UNDER NUTRITION AND OVERWEIGHT)

National development is largely dependent on healthy and well-nourished people. However, there are many children who are not always able to access sufficient, safe, nutritious food and a balanced diet that meets their needs for optimal growth and development. Poor nutrition in utero and early childhood often results in **stunting** which refers to a child who is too short for his or her age. Similarly **wasting,** a child who is too thin for his or her height, is usually the result form a poor diet and/or disease. Stunting and wasting often lead to noticeable educational and economic disadvantages that could last a lifetime and affect the next generation (UNICEF/WHO/World Bank Group 2018). On the other end, **overweight or obese children**, too heavy for his or her height, are at greater risk of poor health and reduced quality of life in adolescence and in adulthood. The UN SDG target 2.2 involves "ending all forms of malnutrition by 2030, including achieving, by 2025, the internationally agreed targets on stunting and wasting in children under 5 years of age".

Many countries in the Asia/Pacific region have a high prevalence of stunting and wasting among children. Fortunately, however, over the 2000-16 period the prevalence of stunting (low height-for-age) and wasting (low weight-for-height) among children not yet 5 years of age diminished from 33 to 24% and from 9 to 7% respectively (Figure 6.7). Stunting prevalence is highest at around 50% in Papua New Guinea and Timor-Leste, while it is below 10% in Armenia, China, Japan, Kazakhstan, Korea, Samoa, and Tonga. The prevalence of wasting is highest in Bangladesh, India, Papua New Guinea, and Sri Lanka. Over the past 16 years, the prevalence of wasting among children under 5 increased most in Papua New Guinea (10 percentage points), Indonesia (8 percentage points) and India (4 percentage points). Countries with a higher prevalence of underweight children have higher child mortality rates (Figure 6.8): nearly half of the deaths among children under age 5 are related to undernutrition (UNICEF, WHO, World Bank Group, United Nations 2017; see indicator "Infant and child mortality" in this Chapter).

The number of overweight children increased from 31 to 38 million worldwide between 2000 and 2016. The prevalence of children under 5 who are overweight varies: it is above 10% in Armenia, Azerbaijan, Indonesia, Mongolia, Papua New Guinea, and Tonga, while it is negligible in Korea DPR and Nepal (Figure 6.9). Over the 2000-16 period, the portion of children under 5 overweight increased by more than 7 percentage points in Azerbaijan, Brunei Darussalam, Indonesia, and Papua New Guinea, while the Asia/Pacific average increased by around 2 percentage points.

Definition and measurement

The WHO definition of child stunting is height-for-age greater than 2 standard deviations below WHO Child Growth Standards median. The WHO definition of child wasting is greater than 2 standard deviations below WHO Child Growth Standards median. The WHO definition of children overweight is weight-for-height greater than 2 standard deviations above WHO Child Growth Standards median. The WHO definition of children obesity is weight-for-height greater than 3 standard deviations above the WHO Child Growth Standards median.

Further reading

UNICEF/WHO/World Bank Group (2018), Levels and trends in child malnutrition, Joint Child Malnutrition Estimates, Key findings of the 2018 edition.

Figure 6.7. **Many countries in the Asia/Pacific region have a high prevalence of stunting and wasting among young children**

Prevalence among children under 5 (%), 2000 and 2016 latest year available

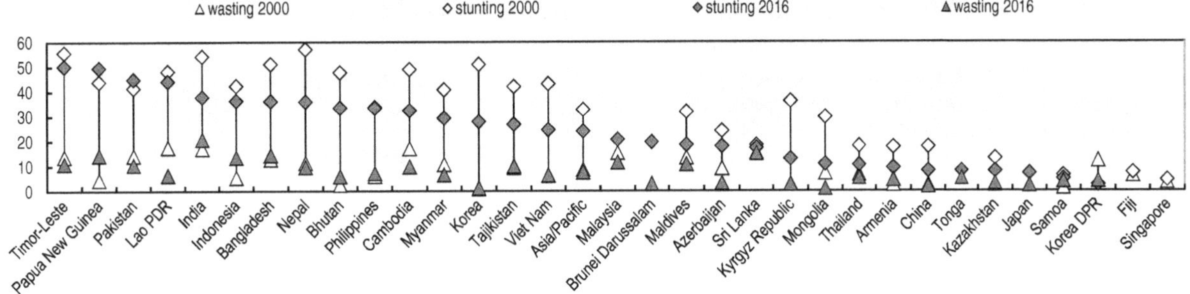

Source: WHO Global Health Observatory data (2018).

StatLink http://dx.doi.org/10.1787/888933900667

Figure 6.8. **Countries with a higher prevalence of underweight children have higher child mortality rates**

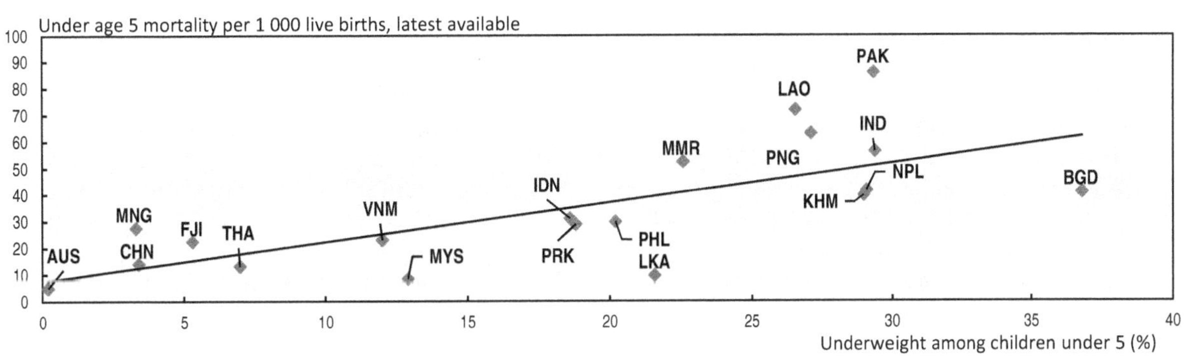

Source: WHO Global Health Observatory data (2018).

StatLink http://dx.doi.org/10.1787/888933900686

Figure 6.9. **The number of overweight children has increased in most Asia/Pacific countries**

Prevalence of overweight among children under 5 (%), 2000 and 2016 latest year available

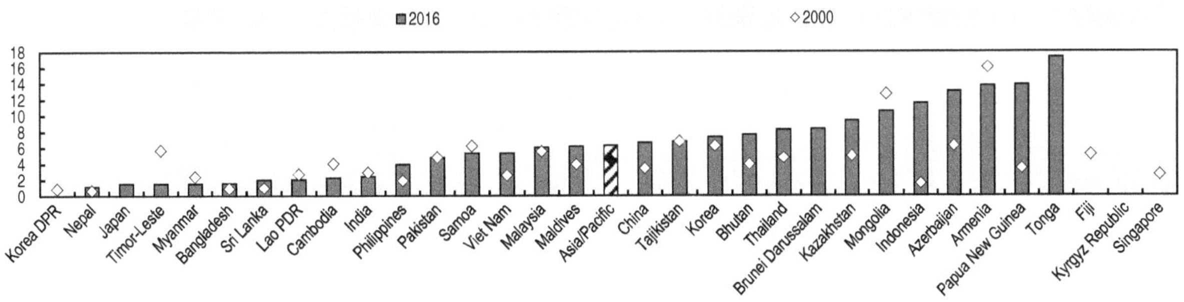

Source: UNICEF, WHO, and World Bank's Joint global database on Child Malnutrition (2018), https://data.unicef.org/resources/dataset/malnutrition-data/.

StatLink http://dx.doi.org/10.1787/888933900705

HEALTH EXPENDITURE

Financial resources for health are unevenly distributed geographically. Australia and Japan have higher health expenditure per capita than the OECD average (USD 3715, 2015), while most of Asia/Pacific economies spend less than the Asia/Pacific average (USD 1 120). On average across the Asia/Pacific, two thirds of health expenditure is financed by governments or compulsory insurance schemes, and the rest is financed from voluntary schemes or concerns patients' out-of-pocket expenses (Figure 6.10). More than three-quarters of total health expenditure in Brunei Darussalam, Japan, New Zealand, and Thailand were financed publicly in 2015, while in countries with a lower GDP per capita such as Bangladesh, India, Myanmar and Nepal three-quarters of total health expenditure were financed privately.

For most Asia/Pacific economies, **health expenditure per capita** grew over last decade (Figure 6.11). On average the Asia/Pacific economies experienced annual growth in real health expenditure per capita of 6% over the 2006-10 and 2011-15 periods, while annual growth in real health among OECD economies was less than 4%. Armenia and Myanmar had the largest annual average spending growth of more than 30% over the 2011-15 period, while Azerbaijan, China, India, Lao PDR, Nepal, Singapore and Tajikistan also recorded growth in excess of 10%. By contrast in Cambodia, New Zealand and Samoa health expenditure increased by less than the OECD average (3.7%) over the same period.

Although health expenditure per capita grew steadily**, the public/private health financing ratios** are relatively stable for most Asia/Pacific countries (Figure 6.12). Over the 2011-15 period health expenditure financed by government/compulsory schemes increased in Singapore, China, and Indonesia, while in Mongolia and Viet Nam saw an increase in the share of health-financing through voluntary health schemes and households' out-of-pocket expenditures.

Definition and measurement

Heath expenditure measures the final consumption of health goods and services. This includes spending by both public and private sources on medical services and goods, public health and prevention programmes and administration, but excludes spending on capital formation (investments). To compare spending levels across countries, per capita health expenditures are converted to a common currency (US dollar) and adjusted to take account of the different purchasing power of the national currencies.

The financing of health care can be analysed from the point of view of the sources of funding (households, employers and the state), financing schemes (compulsory or voluntary insurance), and financing agents (organisations managing the financing schemes). Here "financing" is used in the sense of financing schemes as defined in the System of Health Accounts (OECD/WHO/Eurostat, 2011). Public financing includes expenditure by the general government and social security funds. Private financing covers households' out-of-pocket payments, private health insurance and other private funds (NGOs and private corporations).

Figure 6.10. **Total health expenditure varies considerably across Asia and the Pacific**

Total health expenditure per capita, public and private, USD PPP, 2015

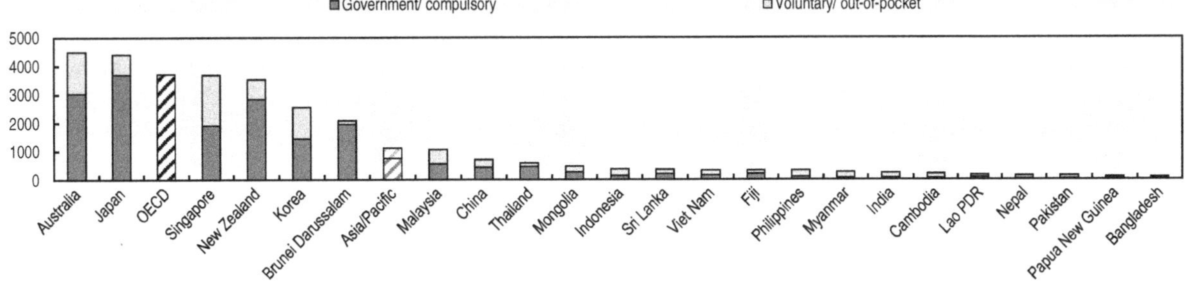

Source: WHO Global Health Observatory data (2018).

StatLink http://dx.doi.org/10.1787/888933900724

Figure 6.11. **Health expenditure per capita increased over the past decade**

Real annual average growth rate in per capita health expenditure, USD PPP, 2006-10 and 2011-15

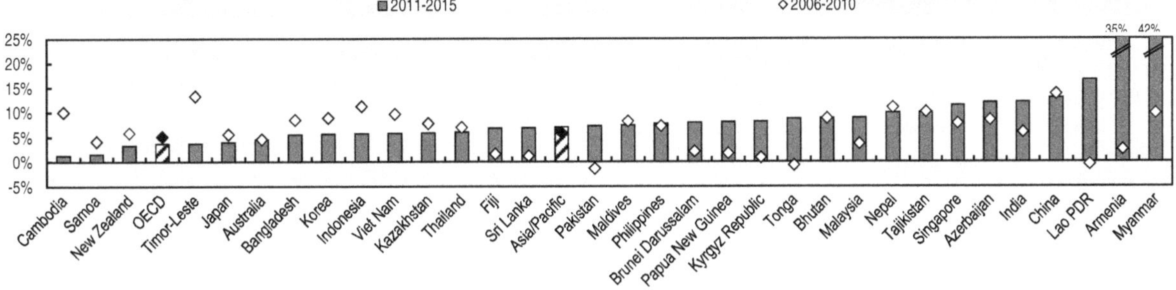

Source: WHO Global Health Observatory data (2018).

StatLink http://dx.doi.org/10.1787/888933900743

Figure 6.12. **Public/private health financing ratios are relatively stable for most countries**

Change in health expenditure, by government/compulsory insurance scheme and voluntary/households' out-of-pocket, % of health expenditure, 2010 and 2015

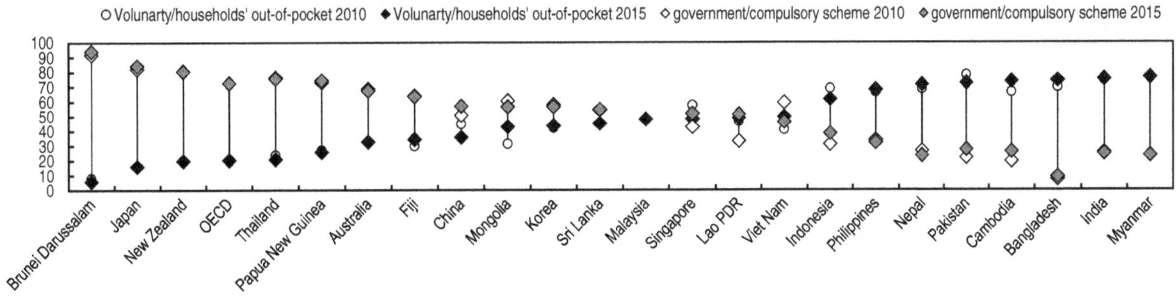

Source: WHO Global Health Observatory data (2018).

StatLink http://dx.doi.org/10.1787/888933900762

HOSPITAL ACTIVITIES

Hospitals in most countries account for the largest part of overall fixed health investment. It is important to use resources efficiently and assure a co-ordinated access to hospital care: the number of hospital beds, hospital discharge rates and the average length of stay (ALOS) are among the indicators used to assess available resources and access in general.

Hospital bed availability varies considerably across the Asia/Pacific region. It is highest in Japan and Korea (Figure 6.13). At the other end, in Bangladesh, Cambodia, India, Myanmar, Pakistan and the Philippines, the number of hospital-beds is less than one per 1 000 people. Over the 2005-15 period the average hospital bed availability diminished somewhat in OECD and Asia/Pacific economies on average. The availability of hospital-beds fell in Azerbaijan and Nepal, but increased in China and Korea.

The hospital discharge rate is at 113 cases per 1 000 population on average in Asia/Pacific countries, compared with the OECD average of 156 (Figure 6.14). The highest rate hospital discharge rates are recorded for Sri Lanka and Mongolia, with over 250 discharges per 1 000 population in a year. By contrast, in Bangladesh, Myanmar and Nepal, discharge rates are below 25 cases per 1 000 population. Increasing the number of beds and overnight stays in hospitals does not always bring positive outcomes in population health. Hence, ALOS is also used to assess appropriate access and use. In the Asia/Pacific region, the average length of stay (ALOS) for acute care is 6.4 days on average, slightly below the OECD average of 7.8 days (Figure 6.15). The longest ALOS is over 16 days in Japan and Korea, while the shortest is 2.5 days in Lap PDR and three days in Sri Lanka.

In general, countries with more hospital beds tend to have higher discharge rates as well as longer ALOS (Figure 6.16). However, there are some: Japan and Korea, with the highest number of hospital beds per population, have a relatively low discharge rate while Sri Lanka, with average bed availability, has the highest discharge rate.

Definition and measurement

The number of hospital beds include all hospital beds such as those for acute care and for chronic/long-term care, in both the public and private sectors.

ALOS is generally measured by dividing the total number of days stayed by all patients in acute-care inpatient institutions by the number of admissions or discharges during a year. The figures reported for average length of stay (ALOS) are for acute care only. In general reported ALOS data cover only public sector institutions, and only a few countries, such as China, Mongolia and Thailand, comprehensively cover private sector institutions in their ALOS statistics.

A discharge is defined as the release of a patient who has stayed at least one night in hospital, and it includes deaths in hospital following inpatient care. The discharge rates presented here are not age-standardised, i.e. they do not take account for cross-national differences in the age structure of populations. The figures presented here come mostly from administrative sources.

Figure 6.13. **The average hospital bed availability has diminished somewhat across the Asia/Pacific region**

Hospital beds per 1 000 population, 2005 and 2015 or latest available

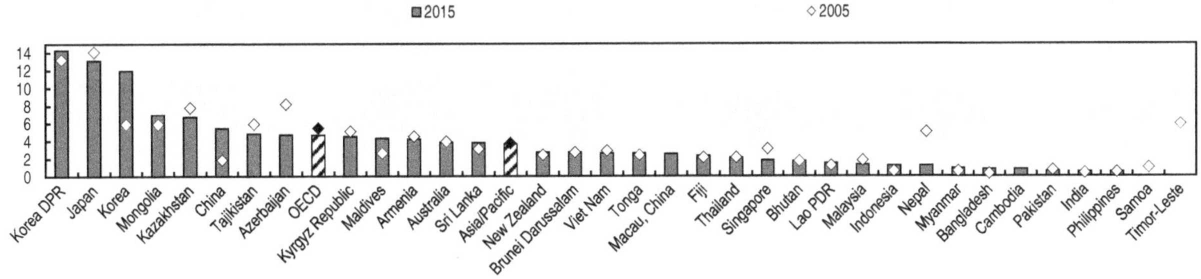

2015
2005
0
2
4
6
8
10
12
14
Korea DPR
Japan
Korea
Mongolia
Kazakhstan
China
Tajikistan
Azerbaijan
OECD
Kyrgyz Republic
Maldives
Armenia
Australia
Sri Lanka
Asia/Pacific
New Zealand
Brunei Darussalam
Viet Nam
Tonga
Macau, China
Fiji
Thailand
Singapore
Bhutan
Lao PDR
Malaysia
Indonesia
Nepal
Myanmar
Bangladesh
Cambodia
Pakistan
India
Philippines
Samoa
Timor-Leste

Source: OECD Health Data 2018; WHO Global Health Observatory data repository 2018.

StatLink http://dx.doi.org/10.1787/888933900781

Figure 6.14. **Hospital discharge rates vary widely across countries**

Hospital discharge, cases, per 1 000 population, cases, latest available

0
50
100
150
200
250
300
Sri Lanka
Mongolia
Hong Kong, China
Australia
Korea
OECD
New Zealand
Thailand
China
Japan
Viet Nam
Malaysia
Brunei Darussalam
Singapore
Fiji
Macau, China
Cambodia
Papua New Guinea
Bangladesh
Myanmar
Nepal

Source: OECD Health Data 2018; WHO Global Health Observatory data 2018.

StatLink http://dx.doi.org/10.1787/888933900800

Figure 6.15. **ALOS for acute care in Asia/Pacific is below the OECD**

Average length of stay for acute care in hospital, days, latest available

0
4
8
12
16
20
Japan
Korea
China
Mongolia
OECD
Macau, China
New Zealand
Viet Nam
Myanmar
Papua New Guinea
Fiji
Australia
Brunei Darussalam
Cambodia
Singapore
Hong Kong, China
Indonesia
Malaysia
Thailand
Bangladesh
Nepal
Sri Lanka
Lao PDR

Source: OECD Health Data 2018; WHO Global Health Observatory data 2018.

StatLink http://dx.doi.org/10.1787/888933900819

Figure 6.16. **Countries with more hospital beds tend to have higher discharge rates and longer ALOS**

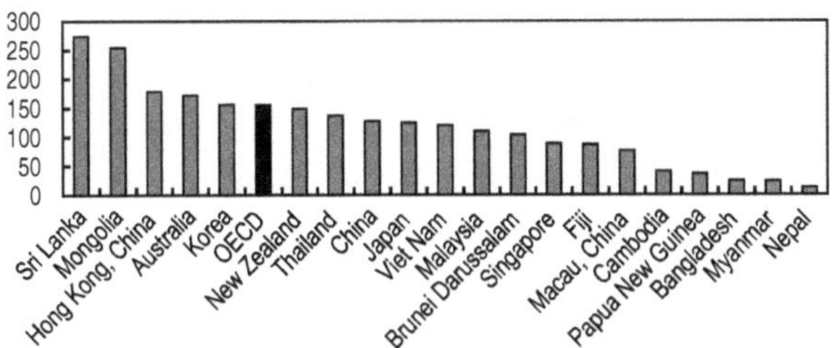

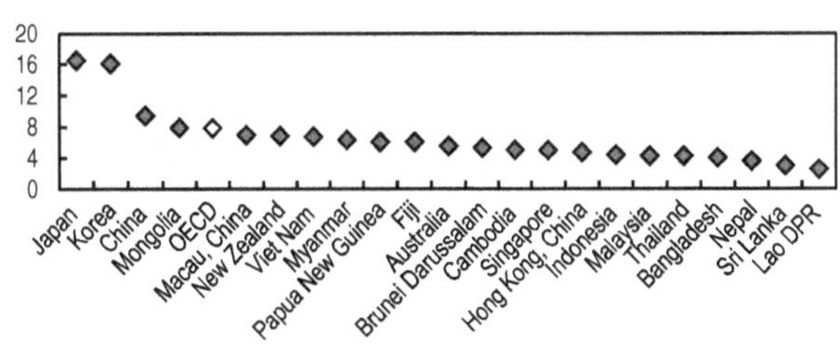

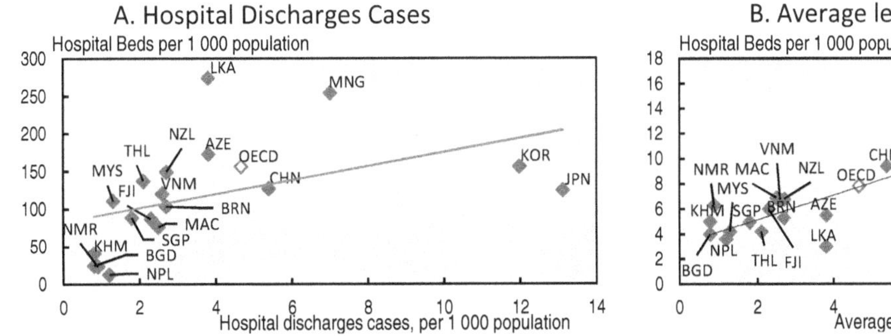

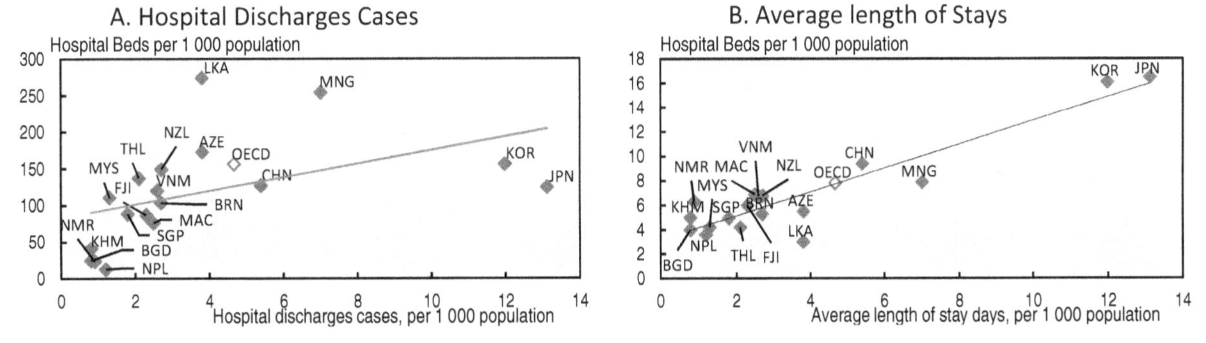

A. Hospital Discharges Cases
Hospital Beds per 1 000 population
0
50
100
150
200
250
300
0
2
4
6
8
10
12
14
Hospital discharges cases, per 1 000 population
LKA
MNG
NZL
AZE
THL
OECD
MYS
FJI
VNM
CHN
KOR
JPN
BRN
MAC
NMR
SGP
KHM
BGD
NPL
B. Average length of Stays
Hospital Beds per 1 000 population
0
2
4
6
8
10
12
14
16
18
0
2
4
6
8
10
12
14
Average length of stay days, per 1 000 population
KOR
JPN
VNM
CHN
NMR
MAC
NZL
OECD
MNG
MYS
KHM
SGP
BRN
AZE
LKA
NPL
THL
FJI
BGD

Source: OECD Health Data 2018; WHO Global Health Observatory data repository 2018.

StatLink http://dx.doi.org/10.1787/888933900838

Society at a Glance
Asia/Pacific 2019
© OECD 2019

Chapter 7

Social cohesion indicators

LIFE SATISFACTION

Life satisfaction represents people's subjective evaluation of their satisfaction with life as a whole. Life satisfaction is associated with good family relationships, health, living conditions and wealth as well as confidence in governance in the broader society.

People in OECD countries are more satisfied with their life than those in the Asia/Pacific region (Figure 7.1). On a scale of 1 to 10, **life satisfaction** scores are about 1 point higher on average across the OECD than across the Asia/Pacific region. Australians and New Zealanders report the highest life satisfaction of the countries observed, averaging a score of 7 out of 10; while residents in Cambodia, Armenia and India report the lowest life-satisfaction scores in 2015/17.

On average across the Asia/Pacific region and the OECD, life satisfaction has **not changed** markedly since the last decade (Figure 7.1, right scale). Trends also differ across countries, for example, life satisfaction is low in India and Cambodia, but while it improved in Cambodia it declined further in India. Life satisfaction increased in about two third of the countries since 2006/08, and the increase appeared most pronounced in Mongolia, Tajikistan and the Philippines.

Life satisfaction scores are broadly similar for **men and women** (Figure 7.2). Women in India and Armenia report the lowest levels of life satisfaction, while women in New Zealand, Australia and Singapore report the highest levels, being also slightly happier than men.

People in **wealthy countries** tend to be more satisfied with life than those in less wealthy countries (Figure 7.3). Thais appear to have a higher life satisfaction than what might have been expected on the basis of their average income, but, results for Australia, New Zealand on the one hand, and India and Cambodia on the other, illustrate the relationship between average life satisfaction and prosperity.

Data and measurement

Data on life satisfaction has been taken from the Gallup World Poll. The Gallup World Poll is conducted in more than 150 countries around the world based on a common questionnaire, translated into the predominant languages of each country. With few exceptions, all samples are probability based and nationally representative of the resident population aged 15 years and over in the entire country, including rural areas. While this ensures a high degree of comparability across countries, results may be affected by sampling and non-sampling error, and variation in response rates. Hence, results should be interpreted with care. These probability surveys are valid within a statistical margin of error, also called a 95% confidence interval. This means that if the survey is conducted 100 times using the exact same procedures, the margin of error would include the "true value" in 95 out of 100 surveys. Sample sizes vary across countries from 1 000 to 4 000, and as the surveys use a clustered sample design the margin of error varies by question. The margin of error declines with increasing sample size: with a sample size of 1 000, the margin of error at a 95% confidence interval is $0.98/\sqrt{\text{sample size}}$ or 3%, with a sample size of 4 000, this is 1.5%. To minimise the effect of annual fluctuations in responses related to small sample sizes, results are averaged over a three-year period, or two-year period in case of missing data. If only one observation in a three-year period is available this finding is not reported.

The Gallup World Poll asked respondents to: "Imagine an eleven-rung ladder where the bottom (0) represents the worst possible life for you and the top (10) represents the best possible life for you. On which step of the ladder do you feel you personally stand at the present time?" The main indicator used in this section is the average country score. Data are also shown by gender and broad age groups.

Figure Note

Figure 7.3. GDP per capita is gross domestic product divided by midyear population. GDP is the sum of gross value added by all resident producers in the economy plus any product taxes and minus any subsidies not included in the value of the products. It is calculated without making deductions for depreciation of assets or for depletion and degradation of natural resources. Data are in current USD.

Figure 7.1. **Life satisfaction and trends therein vary considerably across countries**

Average points of life satisfaction on an 11-step ladder from 0-10

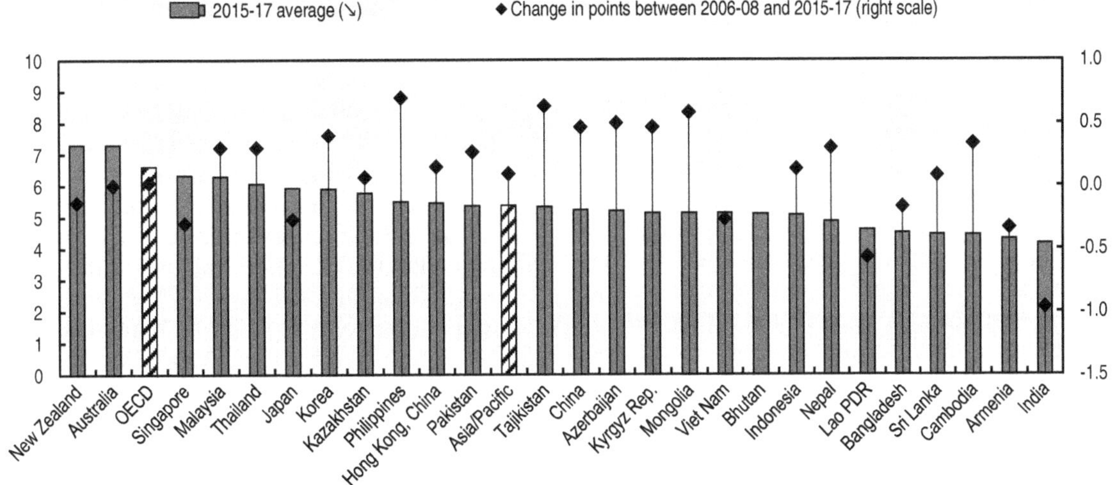

Source: Gallup World Poll (*www.gallup.com*) and World Bank, *World Development Indicators*, *http://data.worldbank.org/indicator*.

StatLink http://dx.doi.org/10.1787/888933900857

Figure 7.2. **Life satisfaction seems broadly similar for men and women, 2015-17 average**

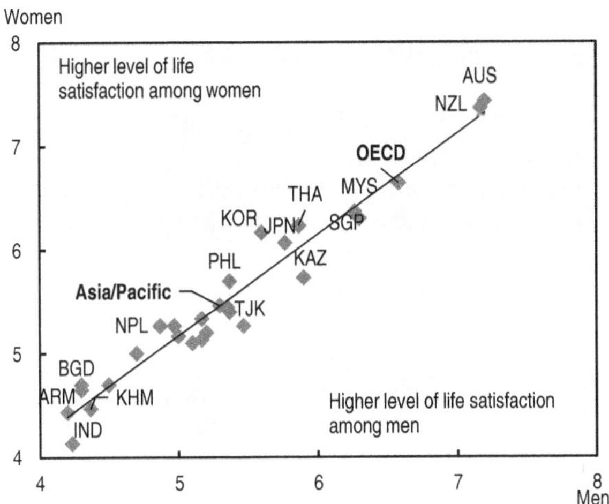

Source: Gallup World Poll (*www.gallup.com*) and World Bank, *World Development Indicators*, *http://data.worldbank.org/indicator*.

StatLink http://dx.doi.org/10.1787/888933900876

Figure 7.3. **People in wealthy countries tend to be more satisfied with life than those in less wealthy countries**

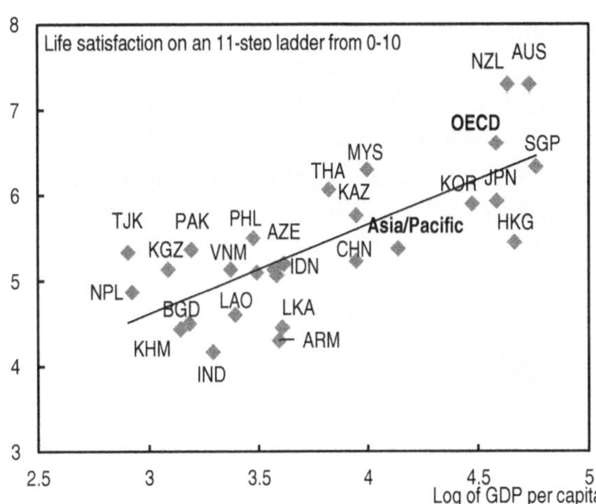

Source: Gallup World Poll (*www.gallup.com*) and World Bank, *World Development Indicators*, *http://data.worldbank.org/indicator*.

StatLink http://dx.doi.org/10.1787/888933900895

CONFIDENCE IN INSTITUTIONS

A cohesive society is one where citizens have confidence in national (and sub-national) level institutions and believe that social and economic institutions are not subjected to corruption. Confidence and corruption issues are dimensions that are strongly related to societal trust.

Confidence in the national government is higher in the Asia/Pacific region than among OECD countries (Figure 7.4), and Australians, Japanese, Koreans and New Zealanders have less confidence in their national governments than their Asian/Pacific peers. Confidence in national government seems lowest in Korea, Mongolia and Armenia. In about half of the countries about 70% of the population has confidence in its national government, and this is over 90% of the population in Singapore. On average, confidence in national government is pretty similar for the youth and total population, but young people in Hong Kong, China have far less confidence in their government than older Hong Kong residents.

On average across the Asia/Pacific region, confidence in national government has **changed little** over the last decade, but there is a large variation in trends across countries (Figure 7.4, right scale). Trust in government declined by about 20 percentage points in Armenia and Hong Kong, China. By contrast, trust in the national government increased among the population of Indonesia, the Philippines and Thailand.

Patterns in **trust of financial institutions** vary across countries (Figure 7.5). Since 2006/08, trust in financial institutions declined with the unfolding of the financial crisis in most OECD countries, but not in Japan. In most countries in the Asia/Pacific region trust in financial institutions increased, especially in Indonesia and Cambodia.

In richer countries people tend to **perceive** relatively low **levels of corruption** in government (Figure 7.6). Communities in Australia, New Zealand, Hong Kong (China) and especially Singapore are perceived to have the lowest levels of corruption, whereas over 80% of people in Kyrgyz Rep. and Indonesia think corruption in government is widespread.

Data and measurement

Data on confidence in institutions is taken from the Gallup World Poll, which is conducted in more than 150 countries around the world, and based on a common questionnaire, as translated into the predominant languages of each country. With few exceptions, all samples are probability based and nationally representative of the resident population aged 15 years and over in the entire country, including rural areas. While this ensures a high degree of comparability across countries, results may be affected by sampling and non-sampling error, and variation in response rates. Hence, results should be interpreted with care. These probability surveys are valid within a statistical margin of error, also called a 95% confidence interval. This means that if the survey is conducted 100 times using the exact same procedures, the margin of error would include the "true value" in 95 out of 100 surveys. Sample sizes vary across countries from 1 000 to 4 000, and as the surveys use a clustered sample design the margin of error varies by question. The margin of error declines with increasing sample size: with a sample size of 1 000, the margin of error at a 95% confidence interval is $0.98/\sqrt{\text{sample size}}$ or 3%; with a sample size of 4 000, this is 1.5%. To minimise the effect of annual fluctuations in responses related to small sample sizes, results are averaged over a three-year period, or two-year period in case of missing data. If only one observation in a three-year period is available this finding is not reported.

Data on national government confidence and financial institutions are based on binary questions: "Do you have confidence in each of the following: In the national government? In financial institutions or banks?"

Data on corruption perception are based on the binary question: "Is corruption widespread throughout the government in this country, or not?"

Figure Note

Figure 7.4. No data available for youth in Australia and Japan.

Figure 7.4. **Confidence in national governments is higher in the Asia/Pacific region than in OECD countries**

Confidence in national government (%), 2015-17 average

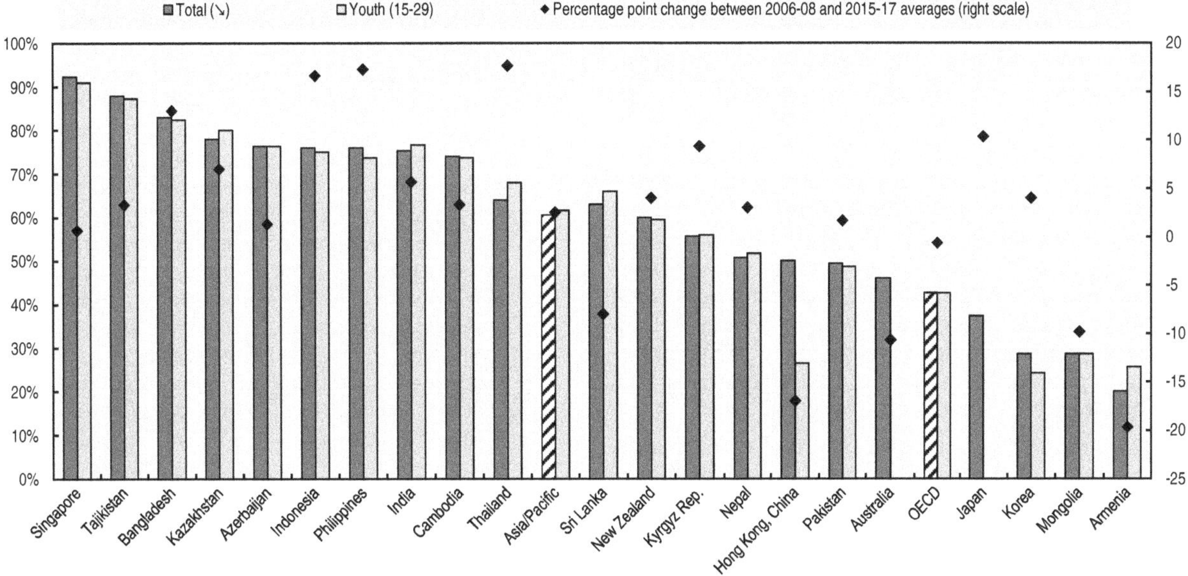

Source: Gallup World Poll (*www.gallup.com*) and World Bank, *World Development Indicators, http://data.worldbank.org/indicator.*

StatLink http://dx.doi.org/10.1787/888933900914

Figure 7.5. **Confidence in financial institutions increased in most Asia/Pacific economies**

Percentage point change between 2006-08 and 2015-17 averages

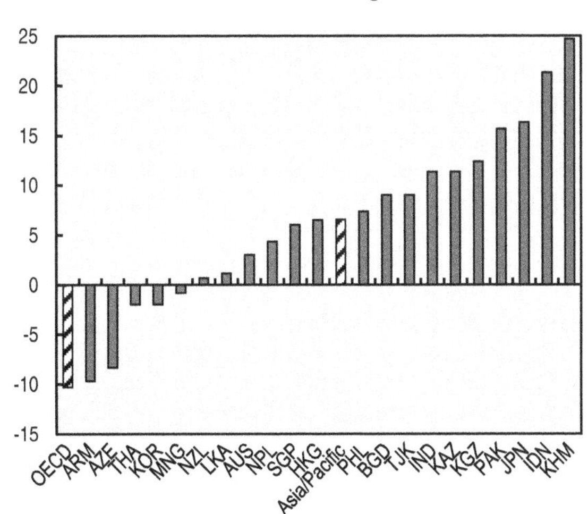

Source: Gallup World Poll (*www.gallup.com*) and World Bank, *World Development Indicators, http://data.worldbank.org/indicator.*

StatLink http://dx.doi.org/10.1787/888933900933

Figure 7.6. **Corruption is perceived to be lower in richer countries**

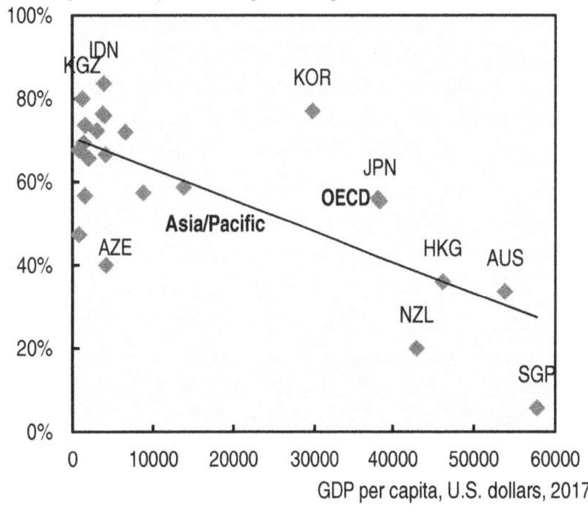

Source: Gallup World Poll (*www.gallup.com*) and World Bank, *World Development Indicators, http://data.worldbank.org/indicator.*

StatLink http://dx.doi.org/10.1787/888933900952

TRUST AND SAFETY

Trust and safety in a society reflects the extent to which people feel that their freedom of movement and their property are protected. A high level of personal trust and safety can promote openness and transparency in society, social interaction and cohesion.

People in general **feel safe** walking alone at night: over 70% of people in the Asia/Pacific region and OECD countries would agree (Figure 7.7). However, there is a gender gap as in all countries women are less likely to report feeling safe walking alone at night. The gender gap accounts for less than 5 percentage points in Armenia, the Philippines and Singapore, while Australian and New Zealand women are much less likely (by around 30 percentage points) than man to report they safe walking home at night. On average the difference is about 16 percentage points in OECD countries and 12 percentage points in the Asia/Pacific region.

Almost 95% of Singaporeans feel comfortable being on the street at night, and this is close to 90% in Hong Kong, China. By contrast, less than half of the population in Cambodia and Kyrgyzstan feel safe walking home at night. Trends in the safety sentiment differ across countries: over the 2006/08 to 2015/17 period the number of Kazakhs reporting they felt safe on the street at night increased by 17 percentage points, while the sense of safety declined most significantly among inhabitants of Cambodia, Indonesia and the Philippines (Figure 7.7, right scale).

The **crime rate** has increased in the Asia/Pacific region (Figure 7.8): on average the reported crime rates in countries for which data are available have increased by 17 percentage points since 2005. However, this masks considerable variation in country experiences; reported crime rates declined significantly in Japan and Singapore since 2005 whereas they increased most in Armenia, the Maldives and Mongolia.

Confidence in law enforcement is relatively high overall (Figure 7.9). Over 70% of the population in the Asia/Pacific region and OECD countries trust the police. This proportion is highest at over 85% of respondents in Bhutan, New Zealand and Singapore. Less than 60% of respondents in Armenia, Kyrgyzstan and Mongolia trust their police, but this is nowhere as low as in Pakistan where only half of the respondents have faith in the police.

Figure Note

Figure 7.8. "See the section on "Data and measurement" for a description of definition and measurement issues that affect the international comparability of data. Measurement issues also affect the comparability of observations on Armenia and Singapore over time. Instead of 2005 the index year refers to 2007 for Maldives and Sri Lanka, 2008 for Australia and Macau-China, 2010 for Thailand. Latest year available refers to 2014 for Azerbaijan, and Japan, 2013 for Hong Kong-China, Maldives, New Zealand, Sri Lanka and India, and 2011 for Tajikistan.

Data and measurement

Data on trust in local police and safety comes from the Gallup World Poll undertaken in more than 150 countries as based on a common questionnaire, translated into the predominant languages of each country. In general, samples are probability based and nationally representative of the resident population aged 15 years and over. While this ensures a high degree of comparability across countries, results may be affected by sampling and non-sampling error, and variation in response rates. Hence, results should be interpreted with care. These probability surveys are valid within a statistical margin of error, also called a 95% confidence interval. This means that if the survey is conducted 100 times using the exact same procedures, the margin of error would include the "true value" in 95 out of 100 surveys. Sample sizes vary across countries from 1 000 to 4 000, and as the surveys use a clustered sample design the margin of error varies by question. The margin of error declines with increasing sample size: with a sample size of 1 000, the margin of error at a 95% confidence interval is $0.98/\sqrt{\text{sample size}}$ or 3%, with a sample size of 4 000, this is 1.5%. To minimise the effect of annual fluctuations in responses related to small sample sizes, results are averaged over a three-year period, or two-year period in case of missing data. If only one observation in a three-year period is available this finding is not reported.

Indicators on trust and safety are based on the following questions: "Do you feel safe walking alone at night or in the city or area where you live? In the city or area where you live, do you have confidence in the local police force, or not?"

Data on crime rates are taken from the United Nations Office on Drugs and Crimes (UNDOC) Database. UNODC collects administrative data on crime and the operation of criminal justice systems in order to make policy-relevant information and analysis available in a timely manner (*www.unodc.org/*). The index (2005 = 100) concerns data on the total number of persons brought into formal contact with the police and/or criminal justice system, all crimes taken together. "Formal contact" with the police and/or criminal justice system may include persons suspected, arrested or cautioned. Cross-national comparisons should be interpreted with care because of the differences that exist between the legal definitions of offences in countries or the different methods of counting and recording offences.

Figure 7.7. **Women feel less secure walking alone at night than men**

Share of people responding they feel safe walking alone at night in the city or area where they live, 2015-17

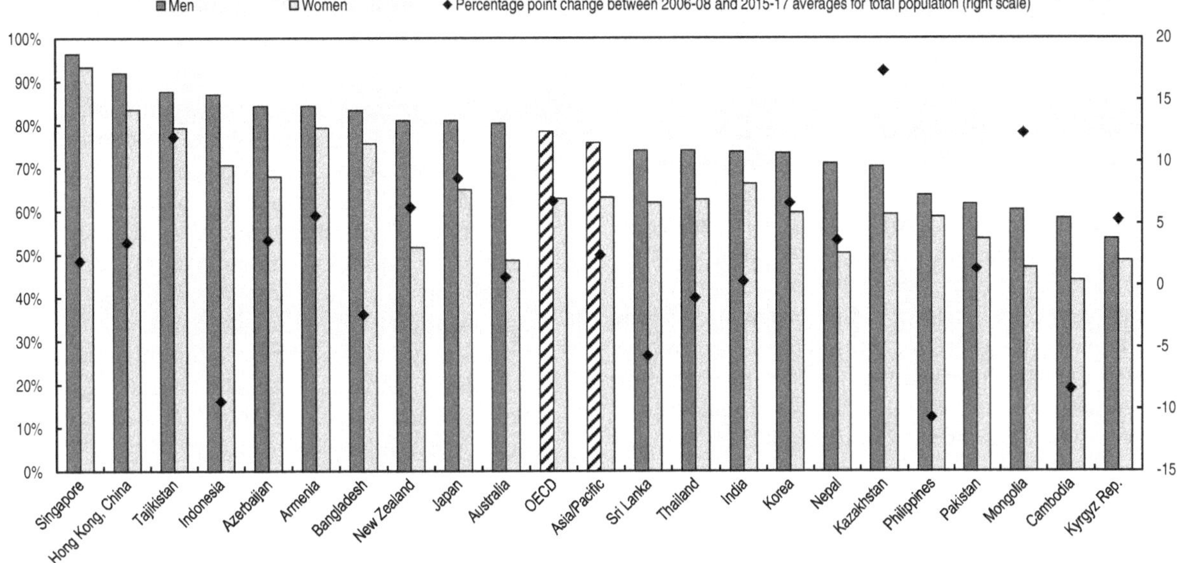

Source: Gallup World Poll (*www.gallup.com*) and United Nations Office on Drugs and Crimes (UNDOC) (*www.unodc.org/*).

StatLink http://dx.doi.org/10.1787/888933900971

Figure 7.8. **Trend in crime over the last decade varies across countries**

Total persons brought into formal contact with the police and/or criminal justice system in 2015 or last year available, all crimes, index 100 in 2005

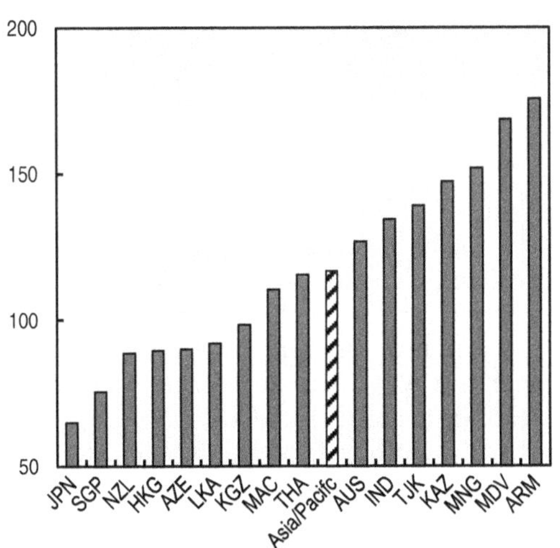

Source: Gallup World Poll (*www.gallup.com*) and United Nations Office on Drugs and Crimes (UNDOC) (*www.unodc.org/*).

StatLink http://dx.doi.org/10.1787/888933900990

Figure 7.9. **Confidence in the local police remains high**

Share of people responding they have high confidence in the local police, 2015-17 averages (%)

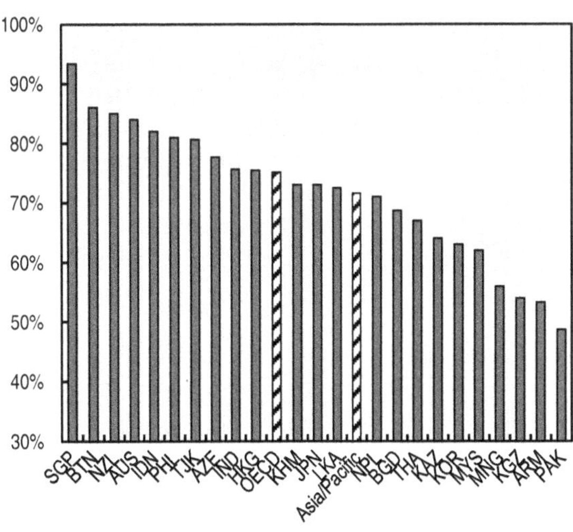

Source: Gallup World Poll (*www.gallup.com*) and United Nations Office on Drugs and Crimes (UNDOC) (*www.unodc.org/*).

StatLink http://dx.doi.org/10.1787/888933901009

TOLERANCE

The degree of community acceptance of minority groups is a measurable dimension of social cohesion. Acceptance of three such groups is considered here: migrants, ethnic minorities and gay and lesbian people.

On average, people in the Asia/Pacific region are less likely to think that their country **welcomes** immigrants than their peers in OECD countries (Figure 7.10). Over 85% of Australians and New Zealanders respond affirmative when asked whether their country is a good place to live for immigrants. By contrast, less than a quarter of Cambodians and Thais say the same (Figure 7.10, right scale). The biggest decline in positive sentiment since 2006/2008 appears to have taken place in Kazakhstan, while residents of the Kyrgyz Republic and Pakistan think their country has become a better place for immigrants.

On average across the Asia/Pacific and OECD countries at least two-thirds of the population consider their country tolerant towards **ethnic minorities** (Figure 7.11). Residents of Pakistan, Cambodia and Indonesia perceive their country to have become significantly more tolerant towards ethnic minorities over the last decade. The opposite trend emergences when considering the sentiment in India and Kazakhstan where tolerance towards minorities is now at a lower level.

OECD countries appear on average to be more tolerant of **gays and lesbians** than countries in the Asia/Pacific region (Figure 7.12). Nepal, New Zealand and Australia record the highest perceived tolerance levels followed by Hong Kong (China) and the Philippines. Only less than 5% of the population in Armenia, Azerbaijan and Sri Lanka report that their country is a good place to live for gays and lesbians.

Data and measurement

Data on tolerance comes from the Gallup World Poll. The Gallup World Poll is conducted in more than 150 countries around the world based on a common questionnaire, translated into the predominant languages of each country. With few exceptions, all samples are probability based and nationally representative of the resident population aged 15 years and over in the entire country, including rural areas. While this ensures a high degree of comparability across countries, results may be affected by sampling and non-sampling error, and variation in response rates. Hence, results should be interpreted with care. These probability surveys are valid within a statistical margin of error, also called a 95% confidence interval. This means that if the survey is conducted 100 times using the exact same procedures, the margin of error would include the "true value" in 95 out of 100 surveys. Sample sizes vary across countries from 1 000 to 4 000, and as the surveys use a clustered sample design the margin of error varies by question. The margin of error declines with increasing sample size: with a sample size of 1 000, the margin of error at a 95% confidence interval is $0.98/\sqrt{\text{sample size}}$ or 3%; with a sample size of 4 000, this is 1.5%. To minimise the effect of annual fluctuations in responses related to small sample sizes, results are averaged over a three-year period, or two-year period in case of missing data. If only one observation in a three-year period is available this finding is not reported.

The results presented in this indicator are based on the following questions: "Is the city or area where you live a good place or not a good place to live for immigrants from other countries? Is the city or area where you live a good place or not a good place to live for racial and ethnic minorities? Is the city or area where you live a good place or not a good place to live for gay or lesbian people?"

Figure Note

Figure 7.12. Percentage point change between 2006-08 and 2015-17 averages is not available for Bangladesh, Pakistan.

Figure 7.10. **OECD countries are more likely to think their society is a good place to live for immigrants than economies in the Asia/Pacific region**

Share of people who think that the city or area where they live is a good place to live for immigrants from other countries

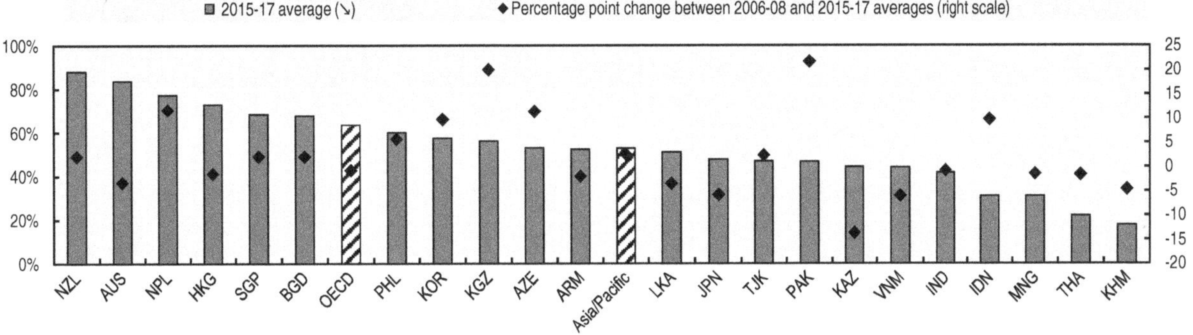

Source: Gallup World Poll (*www.gallup.com*).

StatLink http://dx.doi.org/10.1787/888933901028

Figure 7.11. **Variation in perceived tolerance for ethnic minorities**

Share of people who think that the city or area where they live is a good place to live for racial and ethnic minorities

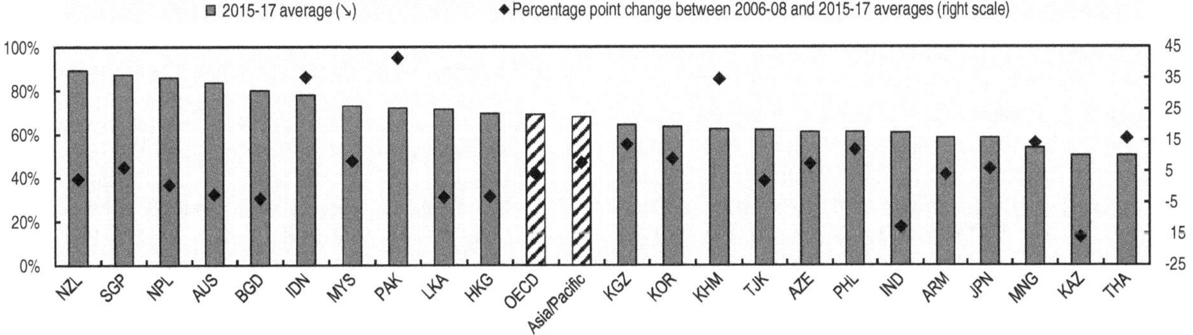

Source: Gallup World Poll (*www.gallup.com*).

StatLink http://dx.doi.org/10.1787/888933901047

Figure 7.12. **Perceived tolerance for gays and lesbians increased in OECD and Asia/Pacific countries over the last decade**

Share of people who think that the city or area where they live is a good place to live for gay or lesbian people

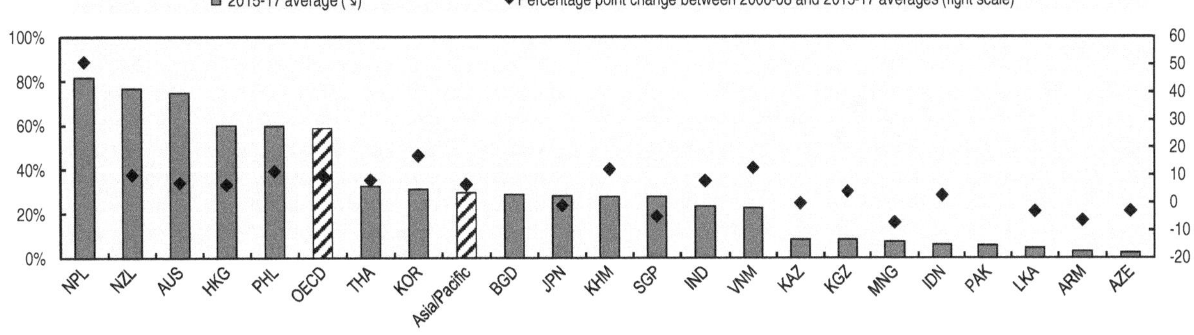

Source: Gallup World Poll (*www.gallup.com*).

StatLink http://dx.doi.org/10.1787/888933901066

VOTING

A high voter turnout is a sign that a country's political system enjoys a strong degree of participation. **Voter turnout rates** vary hugely across the region (Figure 7.13). Over eight in every ten people turn out to vote in parliamentary elections in Viet Nam, Lao PDR and Indonesia, compared to less than one in every two people in Azerbaijan, Kyrgyzstan, Pakistan and Thailand, the lowest turnouts in the Asia/Pacific region. In all other countries for which data is available on voter turnout in parliamentary elections, more than half of the eligible population votes.

Voter turnout has **generally declined** in most OECD and Asia/Pacific countries (Figure 7.13). Azerbaijan and Nepal have experienced the sharpest decline in voter turnout since the 1990s, but since then voter participation in national elections turnout also dropped significantly in Bangladesh, Cambodia, Japan, Korea and Mongolia and Thailand. In contrast, voter participation increased most in Armenia and India since the 1990s.

Confidence in the **electoral process** is an essential element for civic participation of citizens. Trust in honesty of elections increased in most countries across the Asia/Pacific region (Figure 7.14). Confidence in fair elections increased most in the Philippines, Sri Lanka and Tajikistan (by more than 20 percentage points) while the largest decline in trust in the election process was observed in Hong Kong, China.

Men and women often have similar levels of confidence in honesty of elections (Figure 7.15). In some Asia/Pacific countries that do not belong to the OECD, women tend to trust the electoral process more than men, and the gender gap is around 5-7 percentage points in Azerbaijan and Cambodia. By contrast, in Australia, Japan, Korea and New Zealand, women have less confidence in the fairness of electoral processes with a gender gap of around 8 to 10 percentage points.

Figure Note

Figure 7.13. Voting age population turnout, i.e. the percentage of the voting age population that actually voted – as available from administrative records of member countries.

Data and measurement

Voting in national parliamentary elections is one indicator of people's participation in their community's national life. The indicator used here to measure the participation of individuals in the electoral process is the "Voting age population turnout", i.e. the percentage of the voting age population that actually voted – as available from administrative records of member countries. Different types of elections occur in different countries according to their institutional structure and different geographical jurisdictions. For some countries, it should be noted, turnout for presidential elections and regional elections may be higher than for national parliamentary elections, perhaps because those elected through these ballots are constitutionally more important for how those countries are run. Data about voter turnout are extracted from the international database managed by the Institute for Democratic and Electoral Assistance (IDEA).

Data on confidence in "fairness of elections" has been taken from the Gallup World Poll. The Gallup World Poll is conducted in more than 150 countries around the world based on a common questionnaire, translated into the predominant languages of each country. With few exceptions, all samples are probability based and nationally representative of the resident population aged 15 years and over in the entire country, including rural areas. While this ensures a high degree of comparability across countries, results may be affected by sampling and non-sampling error, and variation in response rates. Hence, results should be interpreted with care. These probability surveys are valid within a statistical margin of error, also called a 95% confidence interval. This means that if the survey is conducted 100 times using the exact same procedures, the margin of error would include the "true value" in 95 out of 100 surveys. Sample sizes vary across countries from 1 000 to 4 000, and as the surveys use a clustered sample design the margin of error varies by question. The margin of error declines with increasing sample size: with a sample size of 1 000, the margin of error at a 95% confidence interval is $0.98/\sqrt{\text{sample size}}$ or 3%; with a sample size of 4 000, this is 1.5%. To minimise the effect of annual fluctuations in responses related to small sample sizes, results are averaged over a three-year period, or two-year period in case of missing data. If only one observation in a three-year period is available this finding is not reported.

Data on confidence in the fairness of elections is based on the following question: "In this country, do you have confidence in each of the following, or not? How about honesty of elections?"

Figure 7.13. Electoral participation has generally declined in most countries

Voting age population turnout at most recent parliamentary elections (%)

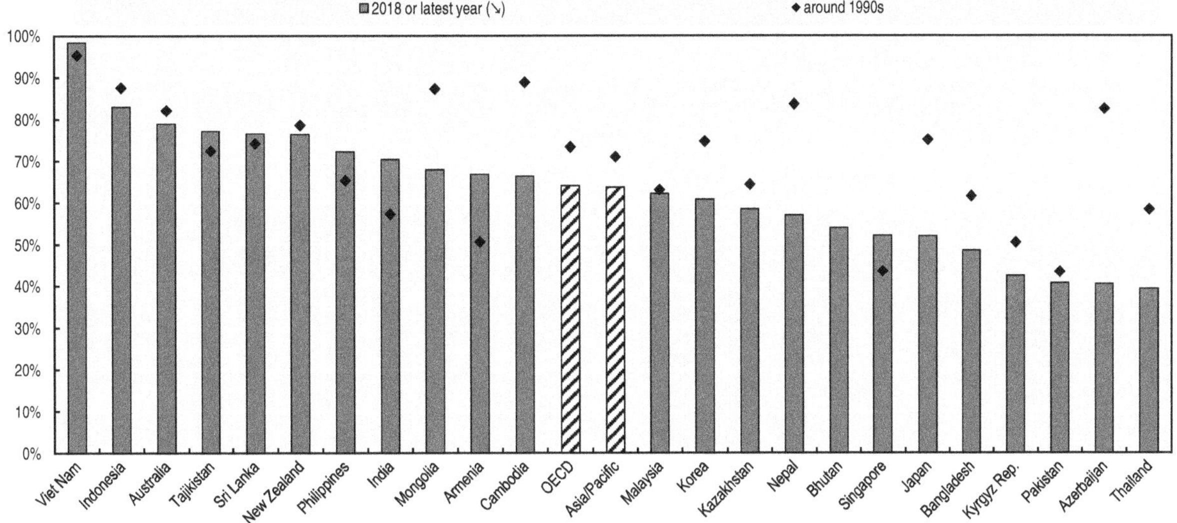

Source: International database organised by the Institute for Democratic and Electoral Assistance (IDEA) *www.idea.int/*.

StatLink http://dx.doi.org/10.1787/888933901085

Figure 7.14. Confidence in fairness of elections generally increased in the Asia Pacific region

Change in confidence in fairness of elections between 2006-08 and 2015-17 average, percentage points

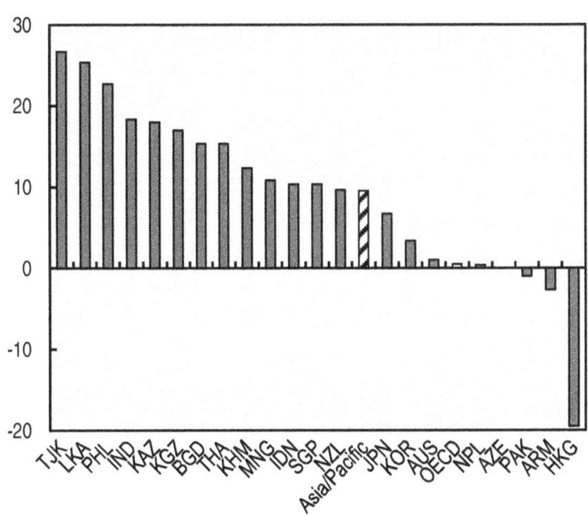

Source: Gallup World Poll (*www.gallup.com*).

StatLink http://dx.doi.org/10.1787/888933901104

Figure 7.15. Confidence in fairness of elections for men and women in the region

Share of people reporting to have confidence in fairness of elections by gender, %, 2015-17 average

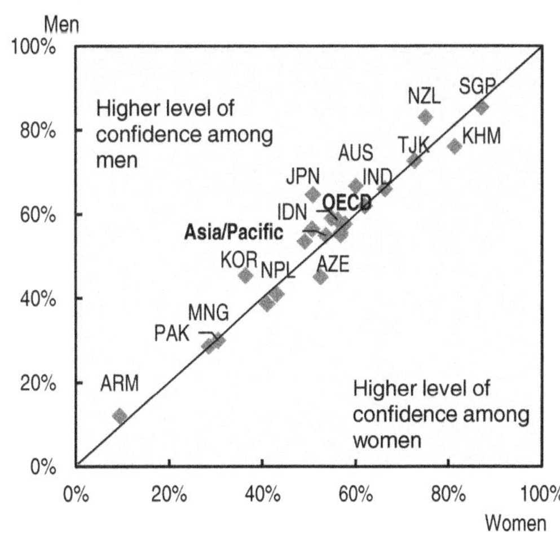

Source: Gallup World Poll (*www.gallup.com*).

StatLink http://dx.doi.org/10.1787/888933901123

ORGANISATION FOR ECONOMIC CO-OPERATION AND DEVELOPMENT

The OECD is a unique forum where governments work together to address the economic, social and environmental challenges of globalisation. The OECD is also at the forefront of efforts to understand and to help governments respond to new developments and concerns, such as corporate governance, the information economy and the challenges of an ageing population. The Organisation provides a setting where governments can compare policy experiences, seek answers to common problems, identify good practice and work to co-ordinate domestic and international policies.

The OECD member countries are: Australia, Austria, Belgium, Canada, Chile, the Czech Republic, Denmark, Estonia, Finland, France, Germany, Greece, Hungary, Iceland, Ireland, Israel, Italy, Japan, Korea, Latvia, Lithuania, Luxembourg, Mexico, the Netherlands, New Zealand, Norway, Poland, Portugal, the Slovak Republic, Slovenia, Spain, Sweden, Switzerland, Turkey, the United Kingdom and the United States. The European Union takes part in the work of the OECD.

OECD Publishing disseminates widely the results of the Organisation's statistics gathering and research on economic, social and environmental issues, as well as the conventions, guidelines and standards agreed by its members.

OECD PUBLISHING, 2, rue André-Pascal, 75775 PARIS CEDEX 16
(81 2018 19 1 P) ISBN 978-92-64-31087-2 – 2019

www.ingramcontent.com/pod-product-compliance
Lightning Source LLC
LaVergne TN
LVHW081411110826
845149LV00010B/1700

9789264310872